Oakland's Not for Burning

Oakland's Not for Burning

by

AMORY BRADFORD

DAVID McKAY COMPANY, INC.

New York

OAKLAND'S NOT FOR BURNING

LIBRARY OF CONGRESS CATALOG CARD NUMBER: 68-55048

MANUFACTURED IN THE UNITED STATES OF AMERICA

VAN REES PRESS   •   NEW YORK

To

CURTIS LEE BAKER

whose eloquent concern for his
neighbors set in train the
events here described

Contents

Introduction

"The Cry of the City"

"Cities in all ages have been condensations of good and congestions of evil. They result from civilization, and are the enemies of civilization."

"The urban life is steadily deteriorating; the suburban life, with equal steadiness, is improving. Consequently, in the districts deserted by good citizens wickedness organizes; the police become leeches on those whom they ought to protect, and government degenerates into a farce. In treating this subject exaggeration is difficult."

"The modern city is the standing menace of civilization—yet without the city there would be no civilization. It is the strategic point in the contest against wickedness. If the city is taken for righteousness, the salvation of the world will be easy; if the city is lost, the redemption of humanity may be deemed impossible."

"Every great city has a voice and utters its appeal. In that appeal are the entreaties of the poor, the sobs of children, the groans of the dying, the despair of the wicked, the wail of lost souls. All these are condensed into the terribly bitter cry which rises from thousands whose hearts are starving with social and spiritual hunger; whose lives are barren of all that makes existence endurable— much less beautiful."

1

Those could be quotations from the Report of the Commission on Civil Disorders made in March, 1968, but they are not. They were written over sixty years ago by my grandfather, Amory H. Bradford, as part of an essay "The Cry of the City" appearing in a book of his essays and sermons, *My Brother,* published by the Pilgrim Press in 1910. In the same book, in an essay entitled "Segregation," he said, "this theory, however honestly held, is the most insidiously pernicious and unpatriotic of any in American life."

Today, this "cry of the city," to which the intervening generations have failed to respond, has swelled to a pitch that can no longer be ignored. This book describes a recent response to that cry in one city. It is written in the hope that it may help others to find responses in all our cities.

This book is about what happened in Oakland, Calif., in the year 1966. In August, 1965, the "terribly bitter cry" of the ghetto of one city, Watts in Los Angeles, expressed in four days of fire, looting, and violence, had made itself heard across the nation. Experts sent by the President to survey conditions in other ghettos picked Oakland as one of those most likely to be the next Watts.

At that time Eugene P. Foley had just become the Assistant Secretary of Commerce in charge of the Economic Development Administration (EDA), which was designed to solve serious unemployment problems in places like Oakland. A year later, in a speech urging that this help be extended to other cities, he said:

Good grief! How many riots do we need in how many cities in this country to sink the point home that our programs for the ghetto cannot all be aimed in the long run? . . . The Negro's sounds of "NOW!" are not irrational demands or threats; they are a cry of desperation; a plea for help. . . . The heart of the problem is Negro unemployment. Jobs are the great need in a land where people are judged by what they do. . . . Unless jobs are provided,

2

... jobs of dignity, jobs with career possibilities, ... all (other) programs are practically futile.

Foley, a man of courage and imagination, used both in deciding to conduct in Oakland a major experiment in the use of Federal funds to provide jobs and training for the unemployed in an urban ghetto. He asked me to help him do it. This is the story of what we found there and of what we and others did about it in 1966, a year in which the framework of a new Federal-city relationship was established. Since then, much of the initial momentum in this direction has been lost, but nevertheless Oakland, almost alone among cities of its kind, has been saved from burning.

August, 1968

Chapter I

Ferment in the Ghetto

"WE HATE Whitey because he hates us, thinks us no better than dogs. Call me 'Nigger,' it gives me respect. I have no respect for Whites, because they have no respect for me. I just want to be considered human. I'm not responsible for five hundred years of history, but for getting justice now. If we don't get it, we'll have a Watts here, and kill and bomb."

With those words, Curtis Lee Baker, a gaunt, tall, bearded, young Negro, wearing a black beret with a gold insignia, tan turtleneck, tight tan field jacket and trousers, interrupted a meeting at the East Oakland Parish on the afternoon of December 9, 1965. Baker, eyes burning, was addressing Eugene Patrick Foley, Assistant Secretary of Commerce for Economic Development, a tough, resilient Irishman from Minnesota, spending an afternoon in Oakland to see for himself what the Oakland Negro ghetto was like, and what he, with the Federal funds at his disposal, might do to provide jobs for those who needed them. John Frykman, Pastor of St. John's Lutheran Church in East Oakland, had brought together a dozen people to tell Foley about Oakland. Jim Reed, of the parish staff, had begun with a general description. Baker, reading a paperback volume of Sartre, ignored

4

this until a pause came. Then he broke in to ask what the meeting was all about and to say that if we wanted to know what he thought, he would tell us. He went on, "What did it cost to bring you rich White men out here? We'd rather have the money. We've had enough studies. What we need now is justice, action, jobs!" He said we wouldn't learn anything sitting around a table, or in one afternoon.

Somewhat to my surprise, Foley resisted the temptation to respond to the angry attack on Whites. Later, I realized that this was wise, as no one would win in this argument. Instead, he agreed that one afternoon was too short a visit and agreed to return for two days on January 7 and 8. Then he took Baker up on a reference to some Negroes waiting for jobs outside the Teamsters' hiring hall, saying, "Are those men still there? Let's go talk to them."

Elijah Turner, another gaunt, bearded young Negro, offered his car and drove Baker, Foley, Eric Lincoln, Negro sociologist from the University of Portland, Bud Karmin, a *Wall Street Journal* White reporter, and myself to the Teamsters' Hall in West Oakland.

There, as Baker had reported, we found twenty Negroes standing around a small fire in a vacant lot across the street, waiting to be called for work as "lumpers," or loaders. We introduced ourselves and spent nearly an hour around the fire—it was a cold, raw day for California—asking questions. The responses were articulate, fair, not bitter. These men held "B" cards for which they paid $8 per month, which entitled them to be called for casual work. To get an "A" card, with regular work and the privilege of reporting inside the hall, one must work thirteen days for one employer in one month. With one exception, none of these men had ever worked more than twelve days a month for one employer. They did not know whether this was the fault of the union, of the employer, or of both, but it was clear to them that the result was to keep all Negroes on the "B" list.

5

While we talked, a 1966 Cadillac pulled up in front of the hall. As the driver went into the hall, they waved to him and told us he was the union Business Agent. A little later, a 1966 Thunderbird parked behind the Cadillac. Its driver was the Assistant Business Agent. No one needed to ask where their $8 monthly payments went.

While we talked in the car and on the lot, Baker's and Turner's angry, aggressive manner diminished, as they felt our interest and concern; though it returned when they described incidents with the police and the "power structure." Gradually, with warmth and humor, they helped us learn facts and real feelings.

From the Teamsters' lot, Curtis Baker took us to his home in West Oakland, where he operated the "West End Help Center," a self-help recreation program for thirty to forty kids, who made toys, bedspreads, drew pictures and were read to. He said, "There have been no pregnancies in this group since it started." Their only funds came from selling what they make and "what they can steal."

We toured the West Oakland ghetto, which seemed better to our Eastern eyes than the row houses of Harlem or South Chicago. They do look better outside, since they are detached houses with yards all around, a real advantage in the clean air and mild climate of northern California. But the over-crowded rooms inside are the same. Most housed two or more families and looked run down, in need of paint and repair. Large areas had been bulldozed several years ago for urban renewal, then left vacant, with no sign of new construction. "They say out here," Turner said, "Urban Renewal is just Negro Removal." They told how after World War II large government housing units for shipyard workers in the island city of Alameda across the Oakland estuary had been torn down, forcing large numbers of unemployed Negroes into over-crowded Oakland. As we passed a large, vacant redevelopment area, they recalled that the demolition contract had been

6

let to a man who had bought a war-surplus Sherman tank, which he simply ran back and forth over the area, crushing the evacuated homes, leaving an indelible impression of ruthless, destructive outside power. Baker pointed out one good, though poorly maintained, park and recreation area. He said that more were needed and that this one was threatened with removal and needed more funds.

At the end of the afternoon, Foley suggested a drink. We stopped in a neighborhood bar—noisy, cheerful, crowded, about ten percent of the patrons White. As we ordered, Curtis Baker introduced us to passing friends. He asked one, a thin, cleanly dressed workman, in his late fifties, to tell us his story. An unskilled laborer, with nine children, he was having real trouble finding work. The day before, starting at 3 a.m., he had traveled one-hundred miles to pick tomatoes, and had cleared $2.75 for the day's work. He didn't have $8 to pay for the Teamsters' shape-up. Looking up at us, he said, "You are all educated men. I'm not. Tell me something I don't understand. I remember the W.P.A. days, when lots of us were out of work. Then there was a respect for ordinary labor, and the government made jobs for us. Any one who needed work could find it. Now the jobs are for those with skills—no one seems to care about common labor. Let me tell you, I'm a grown man, and I can't weep outside, but when I think of my kids, and what they need, and how I can't get work, I'm weeping inside, all the time."

It was time to go. When we had said our goodbyes and got to the car, Eric Lincoln was late coming out. As we drove off, we were relieved to find that he had done what none of us, as Whites, had felt able to do. He said, "I thought that was a good man, and now I know he is. I gave him some money to buy food for his wife and kids, and then gave him an extra dollar to get a drink for himself, which I would need if I were him. But he didn't buy the drink, he just thanked me and took it all to the grocery store as fast as he could go."

7

Curtis Baker and Elijah Turner took us to the heliport, on top of a modern, spiraling garage in downtown Oakland. As we parted, we agreed again to return to learn more at a mass meeting that Baker and Turner would arrange on Saturday, January 8.

At the San Francisco airport, we had an hour before Lincoln's plane left for Portland and Foley's for Washington. We talked of Curtis Baker, of the contrast between his oratory of hate and resentment, and his warmth and gentleness when talking privately and seeking facts. Lincoln, speaking as a sociologist, referred to him as "both a showman and a natural leader," and an example of the historical problem of the ghetto, "which cannot produce unitary leadership, but only many small leaders like this, each with his own following, and often with conflicting aims."

Foley told us that, in the current EDA program, he wanted to attack the problems of poverty in an urban ghetto by providing employment opportunities. He was considering a coordinated approach of all Federal, state, and local programs in Oakland as a test area and would like to have me consider taking this on as a consultant, to put the whole thing together, with Lincoln and his staff as a research team. He emphasized that the main need was employment, but that a way must be found to balance the involvement of those affected by Federal programs with the necessity of dealing with the local "power structure."

After they left, I went for the night to the Pacific Union Club in San Francisco, where a friend had given me a guest card. After dinner, I walked around Nob Hill in the moonlight, reflecting on the difference between these opulent surroundings and what we had seen that afternoon across the Bay in the Oakland Flatlands.

The day before I had put away my skis in my house in Aspen, Colorado, to drive over the snowy passes to Denver.

8

There I had met Anne Gould, the EDA Training Coordinator. Her report on a visit to Oakland two months earlier, which enlisted Foley's initial interest, began:

This report confirms . . . that racial tension does exist, that there is sufficient mistrust, disaffection, and frustration building up in the Negro community to make the situation potentially explosive. This opinion is shared by most of the people talked to, their views differing only in degree. . . . The more optimistic feel that we have a year in which to improve the climate; others believe the situation to be such that any incident can spark an explosion.

During breakfast and on the morning plane from Denver to San Francisco, Miss Gould gave me a good grounding in the problems of Oakland, and what EDA, through job creation and training, along with other Federal programs, could do to solve them. She emphasized the importance now of stopping further study and getting something started, on as many fronts as possible.

At noon we had met Gene Foley and his party arriving from Dallas at the San Francisco airport, and helicoptered to Oakland for lunch in Jack London Square, hosted by Barney Hilburn, the Negro member of the school board, with the heads of the school board and health department, Dr. Phillips and Dr. Malcolm, Ken Robertson, and Gerry Parrish, of the U.S. Department of Labor, and Bill Clayton, the EDA representative on the West Coast. They confirmed what we had read of Oakland's problems: The high percentage of Negroes, over 30 percent, confined to Oakland by the restrictive real-estate practices of surrounding communities, and the high unemployment rate among Negroes—15 percent to 20 percent.

It had been quite a day. The next morning, I sat down and, after completing my notes for the diary I then started, outlined my thoughts about future action. I am surprised at how close I came. I wrote:

9

December 10, 1965

Outline of program

1) Prompt action needed to make start on providing jobs.
2) Problem of involving those affected *vs* "The power structure" (city, government, and police)—both need to be in it, but wide chasm and failure of communication—cf. Poverty Program problems in this area.
3) Inventory of available Federal, state, and city resources
   Federal: Poverty Program
            Labor Department
            Community Relations
            Commerce
4) Comparison with New Deal battle against depression—Watts, New York City, Rochester make ghetto crisis equally demanding, and solutions equally baffling. "Creative confusion" of trying many solutions inevitable and necessary, but it must not impede action. Strong personality in any area can take lead, and others will fall in line. Cf. command responsibility in military, where one service leads and others fit in. Commerce could take lead in Oakland, Labor Detroit, etc., and successful programs adapted for use elsewhere.
5) Importance of point of view. In expanding affluent society, easy to assume that all ultimately share, but ghettos are in deepening depression and crisis, while others prosper—a submerged and hidden depression, unlike thirties when all were affected. Important to see this from the point of view of those in the ghetto and find for them, as individuals:
   —jobs that match their skills, including made work.
   —training to acquire skills to match available job shortages, with subsistence payments during training.
   —ways of participating in the process of getting results,

10

so that it is not "they," the "power structure," or "Whitey" who controls their destiny, but "we".

—example of Detroit's success in training resulting in reduction of relief case load.

6) Danger points—

—How to remove "power structure" roadblocks?

—Labor union restrictions—legal action too slow and will meet great resistance—at what level to persuade?

—governmental jurisdictional jealousies—this is a "hot" issue—all want to be in on success and to blame others for failures.

In a letter the same day, after describing all this, I wrote:

"I have never felt a greater sense of urgency, or of wanting to be involved in solving a demanding problem, and I hope this works out. This would be a temporary appointment, which is good and leaves me much freer to operate than if I had a permanent job in Foley's department, and he sees the advantages of this. I like him—he is a mover and shaker and will be fun to work with."

A month later, on Friday, January 7, 1966, Foley and I returned to Oakland. We met first in Riverside, Calif., to attend a symposium, sponsored by the American Cement Company and Urban America, on the future of American cities. The emphasis was on innovation in architecture, engineering, and construction methods, but these were related to human needs and the urgency of planning to solve the problem of poverty in the ghettos. The architectural critic of the San Francisco *Chronicle*, Allen Temko, offered two quotations which we were to remember in the following days:

Henry Miller: "Newspapers can lie, politicians can lie, but the streets howl with truth."

Nervi: "In an age of general vulgarity, poverty is one of the great incentives to excellence."

11

We were returning to Oakland for the "mass meeting" Saturday morning called by Curtis Baker, to hear more about the needs of the unemployed and to meet others for a broader review than had been possible on our brief visit December 9. On the plane from Los Angeles, Foley said, "Amory, I've got a real problem about tomorrow's meeting. Last night Mrs. Lyndon Johnson called my wife, Fran, to ask us to a small informal dinner at the White House tomorrow night. Fran, who is an artist and not tuned in on Washington politics and protocol, said we could not come because I was in California. This morning my office was on the phone, after a call from the White House, to tell me about it and to say that the only way I can get to Washington for dinner is to take a 10 a.m. flight from San Francisco tomorrow morning. This is going to be a small dinner, only three or four young couples. We have been to one before, and it is something the President likes to do, to keep in touch with younger people in the government whom he doesn't see officially. It is important to me, and I want to do it. Also, it is the custom in Washington that everyone else's schedule must be adjusted to meet the President's. I think I just will have to change mine tomorrow and miss Curtis Baker's meeting. I've been to ghetto meetings like that before, and it's quite probable that only three or four will turn up. You can take care of it anyway."

I replied that I was not a government official and that he was Assistant Secretary of Commerce, for whom the meeting had been called, reminding him that, when criticized for spending only an afternoon in Oakland December 9, he had promised to return January 8 for a mass meeting of ghetto residents and a more extended tour. In view of the tense situation in Oakland, I thought it would be a great mistake to disappoint a large group of ghetto residents who had come to tell him their problems. He returned to the subject several times, but I offered no relief. When we got to Oakland, in the restaurant before dinner, he went to a phone booth. I could

12

hear him putting in a call to the White House, and saying, "Please tell the President I would have to disappoint a protest meeting of ghetto residents, set up a month ago, and that in view of the tense situation here, I am sure he would agree I should stay here and go to the meeting." The subject was not mentioned again, but I thought of it when I saw that the call to the meeting (printed below) began "Eugene A. Foley, U.S. Department of Commerce, President Johnson's Trouble-shooter, wants to talk to you to prevent a Watts in Oakland," and again when I heard Curtis Baker's abusive farewell.

We had dinner with John Frykman, of the East Oakland Parish, and his wife, and then visited two families with Evan Golder of the West Oakland Christian Parish. These two "parishes" had played an important role in Oakland. The East Oakland group was made up of White ministers of all faiths who were pastors of churches in the Oakland area. They contributed a large part of their time to work in the poverty areas, supported by their parishes and other friends. Housed at that time in a roomy former bank in the center of East Oakland, at Fruitvale Avenue and East 14th Street—owned by six local doctors who, when they discovered what was going on there, terminated the lease—they provided a range of services to the poor. The most important, I think, were to encourage various forms of community organization and action, both within and outside the poverty program. In these, residents of the poverty area, who had always felt that all decisions affecting their lives were made by someone "outside"— by the "power structure," City Hall, the police, employers— learned to organize, to discuss their problems, and to find ways of solving them. In addition, they provided direct services in distributing food and clothing provided by their churches and undertook such poverty-program activities as work-study, summer youth camps, and small business development.

The West Oakland Protestant Parish was smaller. Its three White ministers did not have churches of their own, but worked full time in West Oakland, out of a dingy storefront office, supported by a large number of Protestant churches in the Bay Area. They did not distribute food or clothing, but otherwise operated along lines similar to the East Oakland group.

The uniform of these young ministers—all of whom were Whites—was a clerical collar, black soutane, and black or gray field jacket. They identified deeply with the poverty-area residents, mostly Negro, with whom they worked. Their language was often profane, full of current slang, more suitable to the field jacket than the clerical collar. They were dedicated, very hard working, and in my judgment, were among the most effective agents of change in the community. They succeeded in conveying to the ghetto resident the idea that he could do something to solve his problems, by organizing, speaking out, and acting, whether through street demonstrations, the poverty-program community action machinery, or more conventional political activity. Because their approach was direct and unconventional, it was sometimes resented and opposed by many conventional leadership groups, including the more conservative lay and clerical leaders of their own churches, "establishment" Negro leaders, organized labor, and even the new bureaucracy of the poverty program. They thrived on conservative opposition and battled for the Lord. As they succeeded in developing indigenous leadership in the poverty community and as the more conservative Negro leadership moved into closer accord with the militants from the poverty areas, their role became less important, partly because it had succeeded. The more objective among them saw this happening and welcomed it. Some others found it hard to let go and were criticized by militant Negroes as "White colonialists" unwilling to let their charges take over the reins.

We visited two families that evening. The first was Mexican-American. The father had a steady job, at low pay, and the talk was of the poor quality of available schooling and of expected difficulty in finding housing when their home, which they owned, was condemned under threatened urban renewal. In the second, a Negro family, the father, who had been injured in an industrial accident several years ago, worked only occasionally. Both sons, while obviously intelligent, had had trouble moving ahead in school. The older one, about nineteen, was a group leader in the Job Corps at Camp Parks, but did not expect to find steady work after that. Already a father, but not married, he sent his allowance to the mother for the child's support. The younger one had a part-time job, while in high school. Both were ambitious to avoid unskilled labor, which had proved so unproductive for their father, but resentful and discouraged at the prospect of finding white-collar jobs. The daughters were doing well in school, showed none of the resentment of their brothers, and apparently expected no trouble in finding good jobs. Including the children's part-time earnings, the family income averaged about $100 per week with ten to be fed, housed, and clothed. The mother, the strong central figure of the group, seemed somehow to have managed remarkably well on this.

Back at the East Oakland Parish, at 10 p.m. we listened to the briefing of a group of White ministers, dressed in rough work clothes, about to "take the plunge," and spend 24 hours in the Oakland ghetto, with $2, as if they were newly arrived unemployed trying to find a job, food, and lodging.

Saturday, January 8, was the day of Curtis Baker's "mass meeting" at the Recreation Center of Campbell Village, a government housing project, in West Oakland, at the edge of an industrial area under the freeway. The call for the meeting (possibly prepared by one of the West Oakland Christian Parish ministers) read as on the next page:

Our taxis pulled up at ten in the morning to find Baker and a handful of others in agitated conversation. It was a gray, overcast morning, chilly for California, about 48 degrees, raining lightly. Baker still wore the black beret, but now the rest of his costume was also black and included a cape made from

LET'S TALK ABOUT PROBLEMS

EUGENE A. FOLEY, U.S. DEPARTMENT OF COMMERCE, PRESIDENT JOHNSON'S TROUBLESHOOTER, WANTS TO TALK TO YOU TO PREVENT A WATTS IN OAKLAND.

Mr. Foley is sent to Oakland to get your real, down to earth, true feelings concerning problems in Oakland. He does not want to talk to the city officials, but he wants you to express your feelings. Everyone who is tired of promises of your city government and the federal government, the following problems will be discussed:

A. *UNEMPLOYMENT PROBLEMS IN OAKLAND*

Discrimination by all of the following:

1. Trucking companies, packing companies, auto dealers association.
2. Downtown merchants association.
3. Problems of farm workers.
4. Lack of on-the-job training for Negroes and other minority race people.
5. Firms with federal contracts.
6. Firms doing business with the city.

B. *POVERTY PROGRAM*

1. Problems of the old aged.
2. It does not benefit the unskilled worker.
3. Many people with police records are excluded from the Poverty Program and other jobs.
4. The truth about the War on Poverty Program.

C. *WELFARE*

1. The attitude of the Welfare Department towards people who qualify for welfare assistance.

D. *SCHOOLS*

1. Attitude of teachers toward students from depressed areas.
2. Better schools in depressed areas.
3. Better and more recreation facilities in the depressed areas.

E. *CITY GOVERNMENT POLICIES*

1. Better streets (more lights) in depressed areas.
2. Attitude of the police towards Negroes and other minority race peoples.
3. More minority race representation in the city government.
4. Removal of federal funds from city officials whose attitude toward the depressed areas is negative.

F. *HOUSING*

1. Slum lords.
2. Redevelopment—relocation of people who have to move because of redevelopment.
3. More good, low cost housing.
4. Rent subsidy.

MEETING SPONSORED BY: WESTERN END HELP CENTER, WEST OAKLAND CHRISTIAN PARISH, AND CORE.

an academic gown, cut off at the hips, with the doctorate's three velvet bands on the sleeve, and a heavy black cane. With angry, hurt expressions, they showed us the sign on the locked door of the Recreation Hall: "CLOSED FOR PAINTING." They had reserved the hall two weeks before and assumed that its closing was persecution by the "power structure" in City Hall and by the Mayor. "That's Houlihan again, he hates us." We wondered, privately, if it wasn't just inefficient bureaucracy, with the department in charge of painting not bothering to check with the department in charge of reservations. A social worker volunteered to get on the telephone and find someone with a key, which took a while because it was Saturday. The audience had increased to about twenty, and Foley suggested that we start the meeting anyway, outside in the rain.

Curtis Baker mounted the steps of the hall and began with an impassioned, angry oration. Foley gently cut him off, saying that he had come to hear directly from the unemployed about their problems. Instead of mounting the platform, he moved about on the grass, asking each individual for his or her ideas. This worked well. Thoughts were expressed frankly and easily. I noted then something that surprised me, but which has since been confirmed again and again. The poor and the unemployed see their problems more clearly, and better understand the mechanisms of society that create their problems, than the great majority of outside, trained experts whose job it is to provide solutions. Also, even when illiterate, they express their knowledge with a simple clarity and force, unencumbered by complicated theory, which cuts through many useless preconceptions. The Poverty Program's standard for Community Action Programs, of "maximum feasible participation of the poor" is not, in my view, a generous gesture, or a theoretical approach, but plain, hard common sense, and the best way for the program to find out what it is all about.

As we talked in the gentle rain under a gray sky, a police patrol car went slowly, several times, around the block, just looking us over, not stopping to inquire, or to offer help. As we felt the tensions this brought to our group and heard the muttered imprecations, I thought how much the introduction of the "prowl car" had done to widen the gulf between police and people. A foot patrolman, like the one who used to break up our simulated trench warfare in new building excavations in Providence, R.I., in the early 1920s, would have had to walk up to us, idly swinging his billy and ask what the problem was. He would have been a man who talked, not a machine that prowled, and when he had learned our business, would surely have left behind a feeling of understanding instead of the strong hostility we all felt in the wake of the silent car.

Soon someone appeared with the key, and we all set to, removing paint cans and ladders and bringing out chairs and tables. The total was now about fifty, mostly Negroes, either unemployed or employed in unskilled work. There were a few Mexican-Americans and, as at all such meetings, a sprinkling of social workers and students from Berkeley, mostly White. There was about an equal number of men and women. Ages ranged from teen-age gang members with exotic hairdos and jackets, to a grizzled patriarch who spoke like an Old Testament prophet.

Sitting at a table beside Curtis Baker, Gene Foley continued his questioning in an easy, relaxed way. The audience responded eagerly. The main ideas expressed were:

—Enforcement of fair employment laws and clauses is needed. Many examples were given of discrimination against Negroes by particular companies and particular local unions.

—Negroes are not represented in employment agencies or union hiring halls and should be.

—Training programs should be set up for all the new con-

18

struction jobs for the Bay Area Rapid Transit ($1 billion of construction) and its future operation and union barriers removed.

—Big employers should provide training for real jobs, at good wages.

—Job training is no good unless there is a job at the end of it.

—Negro employers, like small truckers, need government loans to expand.

—Police records are a bar to many jobs where they should not be.

—Mark Comfort, a young Negro who wore a beret like Curtis Baker's and a large gold earring in one ear, made an eloquent, strong statement on the need for action now which would produce training and jobs. Instead of threatening a Watts riot here, he simply emphasized that the frustrations, tensions, and needs were so great that an explosion was inevitable unless prompt action was taken. His bearing and manner showed real qualities of leadership, and we were not surprised to learn later that his work with street gangs and at the Youth Corps training center had been unusually effective.

—The ancient prophet referred to what the government was doing for Cuban refugees, and said, "We hewed the forest, we laid the rails, we built this western land. Don't we deserve as much help as newcomers?"

—An older woman said, "Mr. Foley, when you go back to Washington, leave someone here to take care of us. Jesus left a confidant."

—One of the Berkeley students attempted to get Foley to be specific as to what EDA would do to solve Oakland's problems. Foley explained that this visit was purely exploratory, and that further study would be needed before any decisions were taken. Under pressure, he agreed to write a letter within two weeks, summing up his reaction to what he had learned.

At the end, in response to several questions about the slowness in enforcing the fair employment provisions of the new Federal Civil Rights Act, Foley explained that this was not his responsibility, and that the enforcement agency, the Equal Employment Opportunities Commission, needed time to get organized and to establish field offices throughout the country.

He then closed off further questions and turned the meeting over to Curtis Baker for a final word. Baker rose, eyes flashing, and said directly to him:

"Let me tell you something, Foley. I have a draft card. If I get a notice, and don't report, I go to jail. Some of these people earn enough to pay taxes; if they don't pay, they go to jail. There are all these laws against discrimination, not just the new law, but state laws, old Federal laws. We all know that lots of employers discriminate against us, but do any of them go to jail for it? No!

"Foley, when you make excuses for that, you sound just like all those other bureaucrats that come out here. If you can't do better than that, you can just drag your White ass back to Washington and keep it there!"

Thinking of the plane he had not taken that morning, I watched Foley redden. Instead of responding, he stood up smiling as if he had been paid a compliment, and began to shake hands and say goodbye to the many well-wishers who came up from the audience. When we got out to the car, I expressed admiration for the way he had kept his temper, doubting if I could have done the same. He said, "Look, this was Curtis's meeting. He was sitting there beside me when I made a stupid bureaucratic excuse for Frank Roosevelt's Commission. I knew he had to disassociate himself from this, and from me, and establish his own position with his people. That is why I turned the meeting back to him at the end. He might have used a politer way, but that is his style. He had to show that he could tell me off somehow, though I didn't need to give him such a good excuse."

20

We lunched with Mike Claxton, a young Kaiser executive, and two lawyers, Rod Duncan and Nick Petris, both running in the Democratic primaries, for the State Assembly and Senate. They provided a good analysis of Oakland's problems, particularly in relation to planning for economic growth, referring to major opportunities which had been missed when the General Motors plant moved out, and a Cabot, Cabot and Forbes proposal for the port's industrial park was turned down.

In the early afternoon we attended two meetings in East Oakland homes, where the discussions centered on immediate needs, such as jobs, better schools, street lighting, street sweeping, recreation, and housing. We noted that to those without jobs, that was the only real problem. For those who had steady jobs, the other issues became important. At the end of the last meeting, a dark, heavyset man who had been standing in the corner broke in to say, "I'm a simple man, with no education. But I know what a man needs most is a steady job. When he has that, he is a man, and then he can pay for these other things like housing, and schools, and recreation. I'm an Indian from North Dakota. I'm a miner. I work in tunnels. When I first came here, I didn't have a steady job, and when I was out of work, I went back to North Dakota. Now I have a steady job, and own a home, and brought my family. There is a lot of tunnel work now, and I get jobs for others. But before I take a man in the tunnel with me, I want to make sure he knows the job and knows what to do. It's dangerous work. But a steady job that pays well, that's all anyone needs."

At the end of the afternoon we had a drink with Robert S. Ash, Executive Secretary of the Alameda County Central Labor Council, a wise, tough, and experienced man who was to prove a strong ally at many times in the months ahead and a skillful antagonist at others, but who could always be counted on for frank and honest talk and sympathetic understanding. He was harsh about the mistakes he felt the State Employment

21

Service was making in setting up the new Skills Center, because he felt there were not enough openings in the fields in which they planned to train, but said labor would support training that did lead to job openings. He was sound about eliminating discrimination by unions, but warned that he could not speak for the Building Trades Council.

We ended the day with a pleasant dinner at Oakland's Trader Vic's, the original one that started this successful chain. On the way to the airport, we talked of Oakland and what could be done there. In a letter the next day I wrote:

"Foley is going to make Oakland a pilot project in concentrating all Federal resources to create new jobs by bringing in new business, public works, training, and ending discrimination in hiring. He wants me to head this up, negotiating with business and labor and all groups involved, and coordinating the efforts of all government agencies." After referring to another job I was considering, which offered both "security and great interest," I said:

"The Oakland job is temporary, but cries out for action of the kind I think I can provide. The simple, brave words of the families we visited, of the men unemployed through circumstances or discrimination, had a deep effect. It is so close and cut so deep, that I am consciously avoiding judgment until after Wednesday, though I expect, then, I will decide to take the plunge on this, and see what good I can do, and worry about the future after that when it comes."

Chapter II

Federal Challenge and
Civic Response

Five days later, on January 13, I met Gene Foley for breakfast in Washington. Afterwards, back in Gene's office on the seventh floor of the immense, drab Commerce Department building, I turned to him and said, "If you are ready to go in Oakland and want me, I'm ready." He said "Okay," and we shook hands. Then, looking out the window, at the great view past the Washington Monument to the Lincoln Memorial, he thought out loud about what we needed to do. As he saw it, the problem in a city, as compared to the rural areas where most earlier projects under the Area Redevelopment Act, the predecessor to EDA, and under EDA had been located, was one of "management." Instead of trying to process the various separate Oakland projects through established departmental channels, he wanted me to act as his direct representative in Oakland to "put the pieces together" there. "Ghettos like those in Oakland will be with us for a long time to come, and the immediate problem is to make the ghettos livable, by providing jobs and by improving the physical environment." The tools available, through EDA and the Small Business Ad-

23

ministration, all related to job creation through business expansion, by direct loans to business, and by public works development of sites for business.

Foley introduced me to Jay Schwamm, a young investment banker he had retained as a consultant to develop a new "lease-guarantee" program, to increase the role of private investment in economic development; he then turned us both over to Joe Hart, his director of administration, for "processing"—filling out forms, having pictures taken for passes, fingerprinting, etc. I was pleasantly surprised at how efficiently all this was done. In a few hours we completed what, in my previous government experiences, had taken days. We were then taken in hand by Blair Butterworth, Western Area Supervisor, who was to be my principal liaison in Washington. Just out of the Peace Corps, he was one of several very bright young men starting government careers who had been attracted to Foley's operation in EDA as "the place where things were happening in Washington." They reminded me of my generation in the early days of the New Deal, from 1934–1937, who began their careers in Washington moving from agency to agency in the same way. Impressed by their ability and competence in a field I was just learning, I was repeatedly surprised to discover, when they mentioned their college classes, that we were a whole generation—over twenty-five years—apart.

Butterworth introduced us to staff members who reviewed the EDA programs in detail, and also outlined the related MDTA (Manpower Development and Training Act) and OEO (Office of Economic Opportunity, commonly known as the Poverty Program) activities. As the new and uncomprehensible initials rolled out, I recalled that the forest of initials is always the hard part of breaking into a new government job—the thing that separates the new boys from the old.

From these briefings, I learned exactly what tools EDA had to attack the unemployment problem. They were: technical assistance grants for research and planning; public works

24

grants and loans to governments and public authorities to provide facilities for industrial and business expansion, such as industrial parks, marine terminals, and airport hangars; and long-term business loans at low interest. All were available only in areas of high unemployment. Since the earlier program, ARA, that had been continued under the EDA statute, had been aimed primarily at rural unemployment, the statutory definitions, based on average unemployment throughout a city or county, unfortunately excluded most cities, where high employment in the business and industrial districts balanced low employment in the ghettos.

The EDA program was designed to create jobs. Combined with other government programs for training the unskilled to fill these jobs, it had great promise, but it had never before been tried in a systematic way in a city. The training programs in Detroit, where a Skills Center to provide training for a variety of jobs had been established two years before, had met with great success in training the unskilled for jobs in the rapidly expanding automobile industry. The Poverty Program also operated in cities, but too often those graduating from its training programs had no success in finding the jobs for which they had been trained.

At the end of the briefings two questions emerged which were to remain paramount in the coming months and for which there were no ready answers. In the complex economy of a city, how could we make sure that the jobs created by EDA, tied in with training, would reach the unskilled unemployed? And, could a large, experimental urban program, for which there was no precedent, be created for Oakland in the time available?

The pressure of time came from two directions.

The first, which could not be measured, grew out of the immediate urgency of Oakland's situation, against the background of the Watts riot a few months earlier, and the predictions of trouble in Oakland if prompt action was not taken.

In the Oakland ghetto, there was a strong feeling that previous Federal activity there had resulted in much study, but no action. While it would take a year or two for most EDA projects to produce new employment, a commitment to do this, combined with training programs for the jobs which could start at once, could be the action needed.

The other time pressure, which could be measured with precision, grew from EDA's legislative history. The EDA statute was passed by Congress in August, 1965, authorizing an appropriation of up to $500 million each year for four years. Eugene Foley had been made Assistant Secretary of Commerce in charge of EDA in October, and later that month Congress appropriated $300 million for EDA for the year ending June 30, 1966.

During November and December the new agency was being organized and staffed, and in January, 1966, very few projects had been approved, though many applications were beginning to flow in as the new program became known. Only four months then remained in which to process nearly $300 million worth of projects, since any not completed and approved by the end of May could not go through the required legal and fiscal machinery in time to be funded out of the current appropriation which would expire on June 30. Further, if EDA failed to use all of its current appropriation, the next year's appropriation would almost certainly be cut by the Budget Bureau and Congress to a figure far below the $500 million authorized in the statute, even though the unemployment figures made it clear that this amount, and much more, was needed.

All of this meant that the EDA staff in Washington would be working under forced draft in May on projects coming in from all over the country. If Oakland, as an experiment in grouping a number of related projects in one city, were to receive the priority attention it would need to do this well, the Oakland "package" should be completed and approved sometime in April, well ahead of the May deadline for all other EDA projects.

After a busy morning absorbing all this, I returned to Foley's office to meet John Houlihan, Mayor of Oakland. He was in Washington for a conference, and Foley had invited him to come in for a talk. On each of our visits to Oakland, I had urged Foley to check in with the Mayor, but he had brushed this aside, preferring to learn more about Oakland himself first and then see the Mayor on his own terms.

In our talks with ghetto residents, a caricature of Mayor Houlihan had emerged. In their eyes he was the villain of the piece, an arrogant, impatient man who enjoyed representing "the power structure" and imposing its will on those without power.

When he arrived, we were pleasantly surprised to see a handsome, tall, florid Irishman with an engaging manner. He looked around the office and said, "The last time I was here, I blew my top so hard they had to pick me off the ceiling." He didn't elaborate, and we decided not to reopen old wounds. Later I learned that an ARA special representative in Oakland had worked out an elaborate project for a census of Oakland's unemployed, which Mayor Houlihan had presented to Bill Batt, Foley's predecessor as Administrator. Batt turned it down, on the grounds that such a census, though needed, was in the jurisdiction of the Labor Department. That had been why Houlihan "hit the ceiling." The same census was undertaken later in 1966 under a grant from the Department of Housing and Urban Development, without objection from the Labor Department.

Mayor Houlihan gave us a straightforward description of Oakland's problems and the public works projects—port, airport, and industrial parks—on which EDA might help with grants and loans. When he had finished, Foley asked him about his background, and how he had happened to get into politics. Houlihan said that he had grown up in the Bay Area.

27

His father had been a policeman in San Francisco. After working his way through law school, he had become a successful trial lawyer. One of his biggest cases had been the successful defense of a libel suit, and after this the *Oakland Tribune* had retained him to handle libel and other questions. One day he was in Senator Knowland's office on a legal matter when the question of filling a vacancy on the Oakland City Council came up. He urged Knowland to put in someone of ability, since Oakland could never solve its increasing problems with a Council of the uniformly low quality that then existed. Knowland asked him if he would serve on the Council. He said he would consider it if he had a chance to replace the Mayor at the next election, which he thought he could win if Knowland and the *Tribune* would not support the existing mayor for reelection.

Knowland took six weeks to think this over and then agreed. Houlihan went on the Council and ran for Mayor, as his own man, and as a critic of the way Knowland's appointees had run things in the past. Knowland later did support him for Mayor. He had since been reelected twice. Oakland had a Council-City Manager form of government, and the Mayor, in theory holding a ceremonial job, was paid only $7,500 per year. Actually, because of the magnitude of Oakland's problems, the job was a substantial one. He had tried to get the salary increased to a more realistic figure, but the voters had turned this down. As a result he was hard-pressed financially, since his duties as Mayor left him little time for his law practice, and he did not know how long he could continue. He did not want to resume as a trial lawyer, since he had been away from it too long, but would consider a government job dealing with urban problems, or an institutional one along the lines of his consulting work for the Institute for Democratic Action at Santa Barbara.

In bringing the meeting to a conclusion, Foley explained that Oakland was one of the few cities that qualified for as-

28

sistance from EDA, because the statute did not cover wealthier cities where severe unemployment was confined to specific areas such as Harlem or South Chicago. He said he would like to run a pilot project there and suggested that the Mayor set up a meeting of local leaders, to which he, Foley, could bring a representative staff group. They agreed on a two-day meeting to be held two weeks later, on January 28 and 29, at Dunsmuir House, a conference center owned by the City of Oakland.

Throughout our talk, which lasted over an hour, it was obvious that Houlihan knew we had been twice to Oakland and hoped we would volunteer some information about our trips. We didn't. As he got up to go, he could contain his curiosity no longer, and said, "I hear you have been to Oakland. Who did you see?" We said we had seen a number of ghetto representatives, including Curtis Baker and John Frykman. He reacted explosively, saying we shouldn't associate with radicals and troublemakers like them. Foley asked if he knew them. Houlihan said he had seen them in meetings, where they had caused trouble, but not otherwise. Foley suggested quietly, "You should get to know them better. Perhaps they could tell you some things about Oakland you should know."

After he had left, we agreed that he was much better than we had expected. He appeared to be intelligent, which should make it possible to work with him, although he was obviously explosive and could be difficult. We noted that Baker's and Frykman's picture of him was as distorted as his view of them, a pattern we were to find often repeated as we learned more about Oakland.

Foley assigned to the Oakland project a group of young men who could be freed of other departmental duties and devote as much time as needed to problems as they came up.

I joined this group at a hurriedly called meeting the next Monday morning. Only two of them, Anne Gould and Andy Bennett, knew anything about Oakland at first hand. Only

29

one, Anne Gould, knew anything about me. She, I learned from her much later, had told Foley, after our December visit to Oakland, that he needed a personal representative there, but that he would never make it "with an Ivy League, anti-labor, management-oriented type like Amory Bradford."

Foley was out of town, but at his suggestion we met in his office, to show that I had his backing and spoke for him. I opened up by introducing myself, with a brief sketch of my background in business, labor negotiation, and metropolitan planning, and said that Gene Foley had asked me, as a consultant, to "put the pieces together" for a possible program in Oakland. I described in some detail our two visits in December and January. The ice was broken once and for all when I concluded with Curtis Baker's punch line, telling their boss to "drag his White ass back to Washington." Then I covered our talk with Mayor Houlihan and told them that Foley was ready to go ahead full speed in Oakland, with public works, business loans, training for jobs, and technical assistance for research and planning, as a "pilot project for solving ghetto problems."

They responded with enthusiasm and went right to work. By the end of the week we had jointly completed a letter for Foley to send to Houlihan, with a detailed agenda of all the questions to be discussed at the Dunsmuir House conference a week later.

During all our time in Oakland this group continued to work hard and effectively, splitting their time between Washington and California. All were the antithesis of the stereotyped bureaucrat cautiously protecting his career. Their approach right down the line was: "What needs to be done? How can we do it best, and faster?" When the answers were clear, they were all willing to risk their careers and their health and sacrifice their personal lives, to get the job done well and quickly. Something happened to us all in Oakland, once we became identified with its problems, that created a rare combination of shared dedication, excitement, and satisfaction.

30

This puzzled, and annoyed, some of their uninitiated associates and bosses in Washington, until they came to Oakland and caught the fever themselves. Hard to define, it was a major factor in the success of the Oakland experiment.

The team that went to Oakland, in addition to Foley, Jay Schwamm (the other EDA consultant), and me, included seven members of the EDA Washington staff.

Three were in their twenties starting in government careers, drawn to Washington by the idealism of the early Kennedy Administration. In turn they had been drawn to EDA by the magnetism of Foley's reputation and by the prospect of helping to find new solutions to the hard, unsolved problems of race, poverty, and unemployment.

Blair Butterworth, Western Area Supervisor, was in charge of the EDA offices in the Western states, and he was my chief back-stop in Washington. Son of a career diplomat, graduate of Princeton, tall, curly-haired, he had a Churchillian baby face, a slight British accent, and an effete manner that belied his keen intelligence and well-ordered mind. He came to EDA from two years with the Peace Corps in Ghana.

Douglas Costle, an attorney in the EDA General Counsel's office, was a Westerner, from the state of Washington, who had been to Harvard and the University of Chicago Law School. He had spent two years with the Civil Rights Division of the Justice Department in the South working on voter registration. Tall, heavyset, his quiet mature manner concealed a resourceful, keen intelligence and a determined ambition to prove himself against any odds. When Butterworth became fully occupied in setting up the new Western division of EDA in Seattle, Costle took over as my Washington liaison. In June, he came to Oakland as my assistant and remained there in charge of the EDA office when I left.

Richard Daschbach, of the Business Loans Division, was a lean red-headed Louisianan, also a lawyer, who had begun his Washington career as an assistant to Representative Hale

31

Boggs. He had a keen sense of humor, and enough Southern charm to offset his frequent brashness. We all missed him when he left later in the year to become a private consultant.

Three others were of my generation and had joined the government in an earlier wave of idealism—the New Deal.

Anne Gould was EDA Coordinator for Training. Small, intense, daughter of a rabbi, worker with the labor movement in the 1930s, a lifetime fighter in the wars against injustice on many fronts, her zeal undimmed by many battles, she inspired everyone with her humor, indignation, and intelligence.

George Karras, of the Public Works Division, had to borrow time for Oakland from a heavy load of work on projects all over the country. He found it somehow, several times by coming out on weekends, and he brought, to the complex problems of evaluating large public works proposals, a keen judgment seasoned by long experience.

Bill Leland, Assistant for Equal Opportunity, had been fighting the civil rights battle since the 1930s. He had great insight, a wide knowledge, and a delightfully vague manner.

The seventh, *Andrew Bennett,* of the Technical Assistance Division, did not fit into any category, except that he was a curly-haired Irishman who could, and sometimes did, serve as Foley's double. He began as an electrician, became an organizer for the Brotherhood of Electrical Workers and maintained the fiery oratorical manner of an effective labor leader. Navy service in the war gave him a chance to get to college under the G.I. Bill, and he chose Yale, graduating in 1949. Union politics—he was an open anti-Carey man too soon—put him out of his union job, and he then joined ARA, the predecessor of EDA.

The explosive tensions of the Oakland ghetto, caused to a large extent by high unemployment, were what had attracted the attention and concern of Anne Gould, Gene Foley, and the rest of us who were trying to see how a large EDA investment could be used to create jobs there. In the meantime, in Oakland, some hardheaded, practical men, concerned with attracting business and industry to Oakland, had decided to seek EDA funds for that purpose. They were the staff and Commissioners of the Port of Oakland, established under the City Charter in 1927 as an independent agency, separate from the city government, to develop the port facilities, build the airport, and provide sites for industrial growth. This it had done successfully, financing the cost of its projects through the sale of revenue bonds. The recent $20 million expansion of the airport to provide a new terminal and a 10,000-foot jet runway, not yet fully utilized, had used up most of its borrowing power.

In 1965, the Port's planning indicated some pressing needs that exceeded its financing ability: a large hangar at the airport to service the giant new jets; a new marine terminal on filled land to provide the large assembly and storage areas required by the new, containerized shipping; and an expanded industrial park. With these, existing businesses could grow and new ones be attracted. Without them, several large employers now in Oakland would have to move elsewhere, and unemployment would increase.

Monroe Sullivan, a new member of the Port's staff, had been assigned to this problem. When he found that Oakland's high unemployment rate qualified the city and the Port for EDA public works grants of 60 percent of the cost of new facilities that would create new employment opportunities, he saw his solution. He went to work on this right after the EDA appropriation was passed in October, 1965. After initiating the technical engineering and architectural studies so that detailed applications for EDA grants could be filed in February —a move that saved much time later—he worked up an attractive and informative brochure to use in presenting these projects to the EDA staff. By chance, he called Blair Butterworth to arrange for an appointment to review this at about the time Foley decided to go ahead in Oakland. As a result, arrange-

33

ments were made for a full-scale presentation to the EDA Oakland group in Foley's office a few days before we left for the Dunsmuir House conference.

Oakland's two Congressmen, George Miller and Geoffrey Cohelan, introduced the Port officials and opened the meeting with a helpful description of the importance of Oakland in the Bay Area and of the way in which its present problems had developed. Monroe Sullivan made a detailed presentation of the Port's needs and its plans for meeting them with EDA's assistance. These would create much new employment, but the entire emphasis was on the need for encouraging industrial growth in Oakland, with no consideration of how this was to provide training and employment for the unemployed in the Oakland ghetto. It was obvious that any initiative in this direction would have to come from EDA.

On Wednesday, January 26, our group met with Foley to review the program for the Dunsmuir House meetings. When we proposed that the EDA efforts be coordinated carefully with those of all other Federal agencies, both in Oakland and in Washington, Foley objected, on the ground that it would delay things, "longer than Oakland can afford to wait." Instead, he felt that EDA should proceed as fast as it could and let coordination follow later. This reminded Andy Bennett of a story: "When Jimmy Walker was running for Mayor of New York the last time, there was an Alderman who was very anxious to get his endorsement for election. This Alderman had a hard time catching up with Jimmy as the campaign rolled on, but finally, on the Saturday before Election Day, he got his ear on a Staten Island ferry boat just as it pulled out of the slip. 'Jimmy,' he pleaded, 'please say a good word for me. I need your help.' The Mayor pointed down at the wake of the ferry boat below the stern and said, 'What do you see there?' The Alderman replied, 'Just some garbage being sucked along in the wake of the ferry boat.' Said Jimmy, 'On Tuesday, Election Day, just remember, I'll be the ferry boat, and you'll be the garbage, and you'll be sucked right in behind me. That's all the help you'll need from me.' "

Said Foley, "Let's just make sure EDA is the ferry boat."

We continued reviewing our outline. On one point, Andy Bennett said he was for it, but warned Foley that there were no precedents for doing it, and that there would be a risk of criticism. Foley came right back, "There are no precedents in any city for what we are doing. This is an experimental, new project."

Bennett: "You mean, our motto should be 'Think wild?' "

Foley: "Absolutely!"

So armed, we prepared to head west. Just before we left, a small incident occurred that illustrated the local sensitivities that would be stirred up by the project. As Foley had agreed at the end of Curtis Baker's meeting on January 8, he sent a letter of thanks for the hospitality offered, reporting that we had met with Mayor Houlihan and saying that we were coming out on the twenty-seventh to work out a program. He decided to address this to John Frykman and did not send a copy to Baker, apparently still smarting a little under Baker's parting remarks.

On Thursday, January 27, two calls came in for Foley from Oakland, which I took because he had already gone. The first was from Evan Golder, of the East Oakland Parish, saying that Curtis Baker had just come in, very upset because Foley had not written. I told him he had written Frykman and said I would send copies. The second call was from Curtis Baker, still very upset. When I explained, he said, "Golder is all right, he identifies with us. He's what I call a White nigger. I used to think Frykman was, too. But he doesn't identify any more. He never showed me that letter. He'd better not walk around in West Oakland any more. Something might happen to him." I replied, "Look, Curtis, I don't buy that stuff. I've talked to Mayor Houlihan, and I know what you think of him. And I'm coming out to meet with him for two days, because the only way we can get our program going in Oakland is to work it out with City Hall. And I expect to walk around in West Oakland and anywhere else I need to go."

Baker answered, "Oh, that's all right. I know you have to work with the Mayor to do anything here. I have to get along with the policemen in West Oakland to get things done, too."

January 26 brought the first of two severe blizzards to Washington, complicating all air travel, but with some delays, our group all assembled in Oakland on the twenty-seventh.

On our two first trips to Oakland, we had sought out the unemployed, the poor, and those working closely with them, to get a first-hand feel of their problems. This third visit was aimed at the other end of the social and economic spectrum— the leaders in business, in the city, and in the port, the men with the power to solve Oakland's problems if we could provide some of the resources needed. As we had been led to expect, this group was Republican, mostly conservative and instinctively distrustful of Federal spending programs such as ours. It was Chamber of Commerce-oriented and self-conscious about maintaining Oakland's identity apart from the bright beacon of San Francisco across the Bay. What we had not anticipated was that these basic attitudes had been suddenly reinforced by a hypersensitivity to outside criticism, of which there had been a lot in January, 1966. Early in the month, *The Wall Street Journal* had led off with a piece by Bud Karmin, who had been with us when we first met Curtis Baker in December. This article referred to Oakland as "a tinderbox," and "likely to be another Watts." It was followed by a similar piece in *The Washington Post,* and shorter comments in *Time* and *Newsweek*. A West Coast magazine, *Ramparts,* devoted most of its January issue to Oakland, with a long analytical study that overemphasized the city's liabilities and faults and largely ignored its considerable assets and virtues.

In fact, Oakland's problems of race and poverty were no worse than those of almost all older central cities across the

36

country. They were much more manageable in scale, in a city of just under 400,000, than those in the larger cities, and much had been done to seek solutions. But, by one of those journalistic accidents that occur from time to time, the spotlight of national publicity had picked out Oakland as a symbol of the ghetto problems of race, poverty, and unemployment. This was deeply resented by the local leadership, who feared, with some justification, its effect on their business expansion programs. Therefore, our arrival was not regarded as an unmixed blessing.

Thursday, on arrival, Foley and I dined with the Board of Port Commissioners, and met Ed Daly, president of World Airways, the prospective tenant of the Port's largest project, a new hangar at the airport. We also met briefly with Floyd Hunter and Norman Rae of the Social Science Research and Development Corporation (SSRD), whom Foley was considering as consultants for part of our research and planning efforts.

At the end of the long evening, in the bar of our motel, I noticed Foley flush, giving a strong negative shake of his head, as he said goodnight to a member of the group who had been at the Port of Oakland dinner. Returning to our table, he said, "I spotted that guy as a small time 'fixer' the minute I met him. You see them everywhere in this game and have to watch out for them. He just offered to get us some girls. If you want a girl, get your own, and never put yourself under obligation to a fixer like that." Later Foley made a serious statement to the whole EDA group, warning them against anything that might even appear to be a "deal" or being open to any "influence." He said we were handling a lot of money, in an atmosphere where attempts might be made to influence us, and that we "must be like Caesar's wife."

The next morning, Friday, our party went out early, at the invitation of the Port, to ride out into the Bay on a "Hovercraft," an amphibious air-cushion vehicle of British design being used, along with helicopters, to provide a connecting service between the Oakland and San Francisco airports. It was a bright, sparkling day, and the Bay between Oakland and San Francisco was at its best as we skimmed over it at 50 knots, raising flights of duck and coot. A stop at Ed Daly's impressive office at the World Airways hangar delayed us, but helped put in perspective the Port's request for a $10,000,000 hangar to enable World Airways to expand at the Oakland airport.

We arrived a half-hour late at Dunsmuir House, an impressive white-columned mansion in lovely grounds on the edge of Oakland, operated by the city as a park and conference center. We had left the question of whom to invite to Mayor Houlihan. He had assembled a group of about forty business and civic leaders, including the Boards of the Port (but not, strangely, the City Council), the Chamber of Commerce, the Oakland Economic Development Commission, and the Planning Commission with their principal staff people, as well as the City Manager, and the heads of the city departments concerned with planning and employment. When we first saw the list the day before, we pointed out the omission of any representation from labor and minority groups, and last-minute invitations were issued to Robert Ash, Executive Secretary of the Alameda County Central Labor Council and to Judge Lionel Wilson, Chairman of the Poverty Program's community action committee. He and Norvel Smith, the director of the city's Department of Human Resources, were the only Negroes present.

Mayor Houlihan was obviously annoyed at our late arrival. He opened the meeting by saying that it had been called at Mr. Foley's request and that the agenda supplied by him would be followed. He welcomed the EDA approach, "on a massive demonstration basis," to alleviate the unemployment problems of Oakland. These problems, he said, had been created by the Federal government, which had attracted a large work force to the city during World War II, and then cut back its employment at the end of the war, and was now, through its civil rights program, "causing further massive migration of Negroes from the South."

Mayor Houlihan referred with distaste to studies of Oakland by several Federal agencies that had referred to it as a tinderbox and expressed strong disapproval of the recent *Wall Street Journal* article repeating this. As a Republican and a businessman, he was not happy with a Federal-city relationship that would constrict the city, and the city's relationship with Federal officials had not been good in the past.

Then, warming to his subject, he said the city "had suffered from the oral contributions of the people in the streets," and the visits of "the gratuitous activists, and the Federal Hawkshaws" who "come in and embrace the poor. All this has kept the fans of discontent going," and was "stirring in a mudhole."

Just as we began to wonder whether we were being welcomed or put on trial, he changed his tone and said he was "full of hope and desire" for the EDA program of assistance and ready to make every effort to solve the problems as soon as possible, working against the June 30 deadline. He introduced Jerome Keithley, the new city manager who had just come from Palo Alto and then turned the meeting over to Gene Foley.

We had been surprised to find that a reporter for the *Oakland Tribune* was covering the meeting, but decided this was a good thing. Also, at the outset, the Mayor told us he was having a tape recording made, which we said was all right if he would send us a copy.

Foley began by expressing confidence that EDA, in partnership with the city, could demonstrate what a city might do to deal constructively with both economic and human problems. He referred to a new form of Federal-community relationship—"creative Federalism." Past experience with central direction from Washington had shown that it did not "allow for adapting programs to the personality of the community. Creative Federalism requires more and more decisions to be

39

made at the local level, with only policy direction from Washington."

In conclusion, he said, "We are here today to discuss in intricate detail the EDA programs, so that you, who are closest to the problem, can see how these programs can best be applied in Oakland. Our constraint, very simply, is that we must create new and permanent jobs for the unemployed and the underemployed. Here, that means the Negro.

"The question is how some mix of our programs can help permanently solve this problem. This is a legal constraint, and the General Accounting Office and Congress enforce it. We must, therefore, have assurance that there will be some permanent alleviation of unemployment for Negroes, for the long-term unemployed.

"We are not going to be another City Hall.

"We are not going to cover the whole range of Federal programs.

"Our exclusive interest is to create permanent possibilities for the long-term unemployed. We are prepared to concentrate in Oakland in order to demonstrate what creative local leadership, in cooperation with the Federal government, can do.

"The public good is best enhanced by somehow attaching it in a creative blend with private interest.

"The public good and private interest are not incompatible."

As he talked, I realized that he was nervous about this and why. His audience contained those who held the apparent power to make our program a success, or a failure. Much was at stake. Up to now, the Federal government had committed over $40 million in Oakland, without solving its problems. The recent publicity about Oakland would make conspicuous the success or failure of the EDA program, with important consequences for all involved in it. Mayor Houlihan's introduction had overtones of hostility which might reflect the feelings of many in the audience. We did not know any of them, or who might be for us, who against. We could offer money, but they must be persuaded, and could not be forced, to spend it with understanding and wisdom. The urban program we were proposing was, in truth, an experiment.

Foley introduced me as the EDA consultant, "who will spend a large part of his time in Oakland, in charge of the EDA program here on a day-to-day basis."

The EDA program was then presented in detail, in a general session which lasted all day Friday and reviewed in smaller discussion groups on Saturday morning. The response from the local government and business people indicated that they were seeking information that would help them contribute to Oakland's economic growth, without much concern about whether this would actually reduce unemployment.

Andy Bennett began by describing EDA technical assistance as "the process of acquiring knowledge and then applying it to job creation," through planning and studies covering markets, transportation, labor supply, and training needs. He was asked about how this could be organized and how EDA would coordinate with other government planning agencies. He suggested that support might be provided for a broadly based nonprofit corporation, with adequate representation of the Minority poor, but this idea aroused no immediate enthusiasm. In response to a question about EDA's relation to the Federal Poverty Program, Foley said,

"We are, of course, deeply interested in the human development problems, but our thrust here is the jobs. We are not here to play God. We are not trying to cut across all programs. We are not going into the problem of the family. We are not going into the problem of welfare grants."

The Mayor asked if there was any limit on the amount of technical assistance funds and whether Oakland would be given priority. Foley replied that there were "adequate resources to do what can rationally be done in the time given,"

41

and that "Oakland will be given priority. I will personally make all decisions on Oakland projects."

George Karras explained that there would be great competition from all over the country for public works grants, and that projects would be selected on the basis of their impact in reducing local unemployment. The questions, directed mainly at the kind of projects that might be eligible, revealed little understanding of their relation to employment.

The business loan program, described by Dick Daschbach, which should have been of special interest, produced a disappointing response. Many of those present had been involved in setting up the local agency required to provide part of the financing under the earlier Federal loan program replaced by EDA, and most of the discussion related to their difficulties with the way it had been administered.

Foley said he hoped to put all applications on a sixty-day-approval basis, which would be the best that could be done because of the time needed to analyze long-term investment factors.

Local concern was expressed over the possibility that such a loan might give one competing business an unfair advantage over its competitors.

When Foley was asked what kind of businesses could be financed, he replied, "The only ones completely out of consideration are gambling houses, liquor houses, and the other kind of houses." The laughter was merely polite.

Anne Gould reported that, on the previous day, the Alameda County Manpower Advisory Committee had approved the project for a Skills Center, modeled on the one which had been successful in Detroit, to provide training in selected occupations. The Peralta College district was selected to provide training, under contract.

Judge Wilson said he had reservations about the possible attitudes of Peralta College which, like all California schools, was concerned about standards of accreditation. They might

42

be inclined to set standards too high to reach those who needed training most and would have to be "sat upon" to make sure they did what was needed. Anne Gould assured him that a special advisory committee would be set up to make sure that the unemployed who needed training most were drawn into the program.

Bill Leland reviewed all the statutory requirements for opening employment opportunities to Minority groups, emphasizing that this could not be accomplished without adequate training. The only question came from the city manager, Jerry Keithley, who asked, "Aren't we skirting the problem? We are getting a lot of good information, but how do you connect with the long-term unemployed? We still have not heard a formula on guaranteeing that the right people get the right job." We said EDA would work with local people to develop a formula.

On the second day of the conference, the discussion groups on technical assistance, public works, and business loans were well attended, but no one came to the ones on training and fair employment.

Foley summed up by saying, "Basically, we're talking about our ability to make democracy work. I am prepared to set up a pilot project in Oakland, to see if a massive injection of money can create permanent jobs for the hard-core unemployed. We are talking about $15,000,000 and possibly upward if you can spend it wisely in a short length of time."

Mayor Houlihan attempted to restate Foley's commitment, emphasizing that this was a national problem and that Oakland's applications would receive a high priority, but omitting any reference to a local commitment in return with respect to making sure that the jobs went to the hard-core unemployed. He went on, "If you really mean business, we'll get priority attention, and an early commitment on projects, with early assignment of funds. . . . We're prepared to do business, and we have ideas, but we don't want any of the Jim Crackery of resorts and Appalachia, and some of the approach of your people who have been out here. We don't believe here in Oakland that government programs are being administered well. Your administration is not doing a good job."

When the Mayor finished, Foley said simply, "EDA is making its commitment to Oakland with a purpose. This purpose is to provide employment to the long-term unemployed. The immediate need is to develop the strategy and machinery to carry out this purpose."

Chapter III

Who Speaks for Oakland?

FOLEY and the rest of the EDA group returned to Washington from the Dunsmuir House conference on January 30, leaving me in Oakland to explore and report. With time to reflect, after they had left, I began to sense the dimensions of our task. A dangerous deadlock had developed between the Oakland ghetto, which was demanding a better way of life, and the business and government establishment, which was determined to maintain order in Oakland and to improve its economy, but was unable to provide the resources to meet ghetto needs. Without outside help, this deadlock seemed certain to produce an explosion.

EDA investment, combined with available Federal training, could provide the resources and help needed, but only through the development efforts of local business and government. We had said we would do this if a way could be found to make sure that these efforts would provide employment for the unskilled. So far, so good. But two hard questions remained unanswered. How could this be done, and could it be done in time?

During the Dunsmuir House meeting, in discussing the employment question, George Karras had used an illuminating comparison. He said, "EDA projects up to now have been in rural areas, where unemployment was created because mines had run out, timber been cut off, or agricultural methods changed. These provide no guidance for a program in a city. When we build an access road and prepare an industrial site of ten acres in the mountains of eastern Kentucky, there is nothing the employer who comes into the area can do except hire and train the local hard-core unemployed. They are the only people for miles around, and no one is likely to come in from outside.

"But when a plant is built in a city like Oakland, all of its employees may be people who move in from outside, or who commute from other parts of the area, leaving Oakland's hard-core unemployed untouched. Since our mandate is to create jobs for the hard-core unemployed of Oakland, we must find some way of ensuring this."

Since this had never been done systematically in a city, there were no precedents to follow. Our first thought had been that it would require the creation of a broadly representative committee of community leaders, including representatives of the poor, with a research and planning staff financed by EDA, to oversee the program. This prompted me to do something that was a great help to our program, even though we never set up such a committee. I immediately got acquainted with all elements in the community, in as much depth as the limited time permitted, in order to identify the people who could help get things done and to learn the ties and antagonisms between them.

My method was simply to see as wide a range of people as I could, to tell them what EDA hoped to do and, most of all, to listen to what they had to say about themselves and about the rest of Oakland—whom they trusted, whom they didn't, and why.

To my surprise, I found almost everyone willing to talk freely. Part of the reason for this, I think, was that the com-

46

munity had become fragmented into hostile, distrustful groups
—so hostile, indeed, that often it seemed like a war situation,
in which "they," the enemy, appeared as the source of all evil.
As a result, those involved were eager to talk to an outsider,
whose function was to listen, not to argue or press for a partisan solution. I did have something to offer—$15 million
worth of projects to create about two thousand jobs, but I was
not offering it to any one group—only to the community as a
whole if it could find a way to use it well.

As time went on, I was able gradually to suggest alternative attitudes and to bring members of different groups together to start needed discussions. Many others were working
along these same lines, but for me, a conspicuous outsider
with a voice in the spending of a large sum of Federal money,
it was sometimes easier to do, and I did a lot of it.

I decided to spend the first two weeks of February learning
all I could on the spot in Oakland and then to return to Washington to decide on the next step.

To reestablish contact with the ghetto, I began on Monday,
January 31, with breakfast with John Frykman, the minister
in the East Oakland Parish who had first introduced us to
Curtis Baker. Deeply involved in the ghetto, his moods alter-
nated between enthusiasm at the prospect of action and deep
discouragement when action was slow. Early in January, when
I last saw him, he had been so discouraged that he was wondering if it was worth continuing in Oakland. This time, he
was full of excitement about a new action group, JOBART
(Justice on Bay Area Rapid Transit), which was beginning to
agitate for the employment of local Negroes and Mexican-
Americans on this vast construction project. After I had filled
him in on the Dunsmuir House meeting, I told him that one
of Foley's assistants, Percy Williams, a Negro, had said after
hearing of our last visit, "You seem to have met only White
ministers. Aren't there any Negro ministers active in Oakland?
In many other cities, like Philadelphia, they have played a

47

leading role." Frykman named several and agreed to set up a meeting.

As he left, his cherubic face above the clerical collar broke into a grin, and he said happily, "Let me know if we can be of any help. If a street demonstration is needed, we can put on a good one with an hour's notice."

He put me in touch with three Negro ministers, with whom I had breakfast three days later: J. Russell Brown, Minister of the First African Methodist Episcopal Church, who was older than the other two, and cautious and conservative in his approach, but deeply committed to improving conditions in the Oakland ghetto; James Stewart, Minister of the Church of the Good Shepherd, who was flexible and imaginative in testing different solutions; and Herman Farlough, Jr., Minister of the Faith United Presbyterian Church, the youngest, tough and militant in presenting the point of view of the frustrated younger element. After I had described our objective of providing jobs and training for the long-term unemployed, I asked for their ideas as to how this could be accomplished. They urged that we involve people who knew the problem, like Curtis Baker and Mark Comfort, whom the Reverend Herman Farlough had worked with, as well as some of the ministers. They also said that at least 50 percent of any top-level committee enforcing EDA's employment requirements should have a direct understanding of Minority problems. In talking about this, I suggested, "Perhaps the real test of whether or not we can have a committee that will succeed is whether it is possible to put Bill Knowland and Curtis Baker or Mark Comfort in the same room and expect either to talk in a way that the other will understand." We laughed, but such a meeting actually took place only six months afterwards.

A few days later, at the ministers' suggestion we met again, this time with Alexander Jackson, President of the Interdenominational Ministers' Alliance of the East Bay, which included the ministers of all Negro churches. I arrived before

48

the others at the First African Methodist Episcopal Church and chatted awhile alone with its minister, the Reverend J. Russell Brown. He explained that his was a "prestige" church, made up mostly of well-to-do Negro families who had lived in Oakland for several generations. Until recently, they had shown little interest in the problems of the poorer Negroes who had come to Oakland during and since the war, but now this was changing. The Reverend Mr. Jackson, who had retired from a similar church, was now devoting all his time, as head of the Negro Ministers' Alliance, organizing them to take a more active role in civil rights and poverty questions. One of the obstacles to this in the past had been that many of the ministers in the poorer churches had not had much education and no training in social work. The younger ministers now coming into many of these churches were well educated, many at divinity and graduate schools in the East and well equipped to provide vigorous leadership.

Mr. Jackson, an impressive, dignified man, vigorous and well informed, soon arrived with the others, and we embarked on a long, frank discussion, mostly about the role of the Poverty Program's "community action" committees in providing an effective link with the poor. They explained that these committees had been set up in two stages. The first was the city-wide Poverty Council, the official body that approved projects for funding. It included representatives of business, labor, and minority organizations, originally appointed by the Mayor, but now elected by the Council. Its staff was the city government's Human Resources Department whose budget came from the Federal Poverty Program.

Under the Poverty Program, the Oakland Flatlands, where the poor were concentrated, were then divided into four "Target Areas": *West Oakland,* the oldest Negro ghetto, a run-down, partly industrial area cut up by old rail lines and new freeways; *North Oakland,* now in transition from a White to a Negro area, tucked in between the university city of Berkeley

49

and Piedmont, a separate White enclave city of hill residences carved out of the center of Oakland; *Fruitvale,* also in transition, with a substantial number of Mexican-Americans and Orientals, as well as Negroes, replacing the Whites, just to the east of the Lake Merritt White residential area in the center of Oakland; and *East Oakland,* running from Fruitvale out past the airport, in which Negroes had almost entirely replaced Whites during and soon after World War II, a residential area for the most part in much better condition than West Oakland, bisected down its length by 14th Street, the garish "Strip" of shops, bars, poolrooms, and dance halls, where Oakland's Negro youth gathered at night, poised on the edge of trouble.

In each of these four areas, a "Target Area Advisory Committee" of local residents had been formed, with the help of the City's Human Resources Department, to provide a source of information and ideas and to comply with the Poverty Program's requirement of "maximum feasible participation of the poor" by appointing three representatives to the top Poverty Council, giving the Target Areas twelve members out of the total of forty.

The Target Area committees usually met twice a month. Their most numerous and active members were middle-aged Negro housewives, who outnumbered Negro men on each committee by at least five to one. Young Negroes seldom participated. Each committee had some Whites, both men and women, and some Mexican-American men. The White ministers from the East and West Oakland Parishes had been very active on all four committees, helping them organize and write up projects and often serving on their delegations to the top Council.

The Reverend Mr. Farlough, who was a member of the North Oakland Target Area Advisory Committee and one of its delegates to the Council, said, "These committees shouldn't be called 'advisory.' They should be *action* committees. Their members, the poor people who live in the poverty areas, are the ones who know what their problems are and what should be done about them, so much better than any of the other Council members, who are all part of the power structure— businessmen, union officials, Negro lawyers—and just don't understand what the ghetto and poverty are all about."

The others agreed that the Target Area committees were the best vehicle for linking the EDA program to the unemployed and that they should be used and strengthened. All felt that these committees could be more effective if better organized and if more of the poor, especially the young, could be involved. They urged that the Target Area membership on the top Council be increased to a majority, as had recently been done in Berkeley. They expressed disappointment that the Human Resources Department had not yet established effective neighborhood centers in each Target Area and had not supported many "self help" projects originated by the Target Areas, such as providing child care for working mothers.

They were concerned about the new Skills Center program, which was not well understood, and needed to be publicized. In connection with it, they emphasized the difficulty of reaching and recruiting those who had stopped seeking employment and of providing them with encouragement and motivation which would enable them to stay with a training program. They described the effective work which had been done in this field by the OIC, an organization set up by a large group of Negro ministers in Philadelphia headed by the Reverend Leon Sullivan. They had sent a young Oakland minister, C. C. Bailey, to Philadelphia to study this, and they wanted to establish a similar system in Oakland as an adjunct of the Skills Center, supported by Federal funds, as well as local contributions.

The next night, I went to a big protest meeting called by the Negro Ministers' Alliance concerning discrimination in employment in the $1 billion construction program of the Bay Area

51

Rapid Transit. There were thirty Negro ministers, and a few other Negro leaders—no Whites—on the platform. The audience of over three hundred that filled the large high-school auditorium was over 90 percent Negro. After listening and watching this group for some time, I had the strange sensation of looking down at my hands and being surprised that they were White. The oratory was sonorous, hard-hitting, thoughtful, frequently inspiring. The best came from a young minister, W. Hasaiah Williams, who combined some highly sophisticated thoughts—outlining the need for a strategy of alternative "fall-back" plans to be used if the initial efforts failed—with an astonishingly effective delivery. He could have started a march on BART right then. In the audience Curtis Baker, resplendent in a gold cape, usually restive in response to any oratory but his own, stood and cheered longer than the rest, pounding his cane on the floor and waving it in the air.

Later, I expected these Negro ministers to provide a strong focus of leadership, but this never happened. For reasons I did not learn, they never called another mass meeting. They continued to be active as individuals on Poverty Program and other committees, but their only group effort after that was to work out the OIC project, which they did with success, after some initial difficulties.

Aside from these meetings with the Negro ministers, I had limited contact with Minority and ghetto leaders during these two weeks, since we had learned much from them in previous visits, and I needed to learn about other parts of the community. I did telephone Curtis Baker, to keep in touch and to tell him about a long article in the previous Sunday's *Los Angeles Times,* which had included a picture of him in black cape and beret and a good description of his activities. He was pleased to hear of this and told me that he was being interviewed by CBS for a TV show on Oakland, saying, "I have to dramatize myself, and have a style of my own, to be a leader." We talked at length about the EDA program, which he had read about in the papers. Referring to Foley's statement that he and I would review all projects, he said, "As I understand it, this cuts the Mayor and City Hall out of the deal." I replied, "No, we have to deal with the Mayor and act through the city, but we set the policy and will enforce it."

John Frykman had suggested that I see Joan Sparks, to get a different slant on the ghetto from a White resident. On February 8, I had lunch with her at the Good Samaritan Home, a temporary emergency lodging for homeless women and children, which she operated in East Oakland. I found there a broad-shouldered woman, with an expressive face, dealing firmly but affectionately with swarms of Negro and White mothers and children. During lunch, I asked her what her previous experience in social work had been. Looking me straight in the eye, she said, "For fifteen years I was a lion tamer in the circus." Out of work and broke, she had drifted into Oakland five years earlier, shared her boarding-house room with a girl worse off than she was, and decided to start a home for others. With small contributions, neighborhood help, hard work, and food given by Safeway and John Reading's Red's Tamales, she had built this up to room for about thirty in a large house, where she lived with four abandoned Negro children she had adopted in addition to her own two White ones.

A natural leader and good speaker—she had started in the circus as a barker at age sixteen, after running away from home three years earlier—she was an active member of the Poverty Council and the Fruitvale Target Area Advisory Committee. She strongly supported the idea that we reach the poverty neighborhoods through the Target Area committees, but urged that we seek the opinions of others like herself "who are trying to organize in cooperation with the city government," and not rely entirely on the point of view of "rebels like Curtis Baker, Elijah Turner, and John Frykman, who regard cooperation as hopeless and feel that the only solution is to dramatize the issues through direct action." She recommended that I see Don McCullum, a Negro lawyer, to get a more responsible point of view.

During these two weeks, I met several times with Norvel Smith, director of the City's Department of Human Resources. Started in 1962 as a demonstration project with a Ford Foundation grant of $2 million, this had become a city department early in 1965, and since then had administered projects totaling over $4 million from the Poverty Program, nearly $1 million from other Federal agencies, and another $1.2 million from the Ford Foundation.

Smith was a slightly built, intense Negro, who was usually described in articles about Oakland as "wearing a Brooks Brothers suit and driving a Jaguar." While factually correct, this description gave an unfair impression. What struck me most about him was the way, when he was tired or under pressure, one side of his face would develop a tic, and a slight stammer would enter his voice. Instead of being a distraction, this had the effect of underscoring the intensity of his feeling. He ran his large staff well. Some criticized him for keeping too much authority in his own hands and not delegating enough, but this seemed to me to be the responsible course for him to take. The programs he administered inevitably attracted criticism. By taking this on himself he protected his staff and assumed the burden of finding the support needed. The Poverty Program and Ford projects, which touched on all the long-neglected needs of the poor, raised expectations that could not be satisfied with the available resources. They were criticized by poverty-area residents for not doing enough, or for selecting the wrong priorities, and by many in local government and by the more conservative elements in the community for upsetting the natural order of things. Smith's job was a tough one. He handled it well.

After patiently describing for me the complex relationships between the Poverty Program, the Adult Minority Employment Project, the Manpower Advisory Committee, and the

54

Skills Center, Smith took me to my first Target Area committee meeting, in West Oakland, the oldest and most impoverished of Oakland's Negro ghettos. The evening meeting, in a high-school auditorium, was attended by about twenty local Negroes, and an equal number of observers, mostly White students from adjoining Berkeley, for whom West Oakland had become a laboratory in many sociology courses. One woman there told me, "The next time I gets interviewed, I'm goin' to charge a fee. I could get rich that way."

At this meeting, Elmer Homo of the State Employment Service described the plan for the new Skills Center, and received a barrage of questions about how to apply for training, and who would be eligible. I told about what EDA hoped to do, and our need to find a way to make sure that the jobs went to the unemployed in Oakland. A question from one of the Berkeley students started me on a new line of thought: "Can't EDA deny funds, or take them back, if an employer does not follow your employment requirements?"

Oakland's second largest Minority group was made up of Mexican-Americans—about 5 percent of its population, or twenty thousand, compared to a Negro population of 30 percent, or one hundred twenty thousand. To learn about their problems, I talked with Bert Corona, an articulate, suave businessman who served as the Mexican-American member of many local committees, and Jimmy Delgordelio, a tough newspaper distributor who concentrated on organizing political action groups.

From them, I discovered how different their problems were from those of the Negroes with whom they shared the Oakland ghettos. The principal difference was the language barrier, reinforced from within their community by a strong desire to maintain their Spanish cultural traditions—a resistance to assimilation much like that of the French-Canadians in Quebec. The difference in language was the direct cause of the high rate of school dropouts, and both were a barrier to employment. Their fear and distrust of government offices kept most of them from applying for welfare and health benefits, which resulted in a deceptively low percentage of Mexican-Americans on relief.

Flatlands, the ghetto newspaper, quoted a Mexican-American, father of 11:

More than one year I have been here. I can't find a job, a kind of job that I can raise my children on. When they understand me there isn't any work. When there is work they don't understand me.

I was an agricultural worker in Mexico. I came up here to see if I could live better. It's better here. I had no refrigerator or stove in Mexico. Only it's very difficult when no one understands you.

There was no concentration of Mexican-Americans in any one area of Oakland, since the Nimitz Freeway had displaced most of them and scattered them through the four Target Areas. This made it almost impossible for them to organize as a group, and left them as small Minorities on Target Area committees dominated by Negroes.

I said that EDA could provide some help to Mexican-American businessmen who were able to expand and who could provide employment where language would not be a barrier, and that the Skills Center would try to help on language, but that I doubted if we would make a significant dent in their problem. Jimmy Delgordelio said it was better to be frank than to hold out false hopes. He thought the only solution was for the Mexican-Americans to organize politically, first in order to change the school teaching methods so that their children had a better chance of completing grade school and high school, and after that try to solve other problems.

Before I organized my approach to the labor unions, a chance meeting did it for me. At the end of my first day, January 31, while I was having dinner alone at a restaurant in the center of Oakland, Joe Chaudet, who had been at the Dunsmuir House conference, stopped at my table. Chaudet, an ebullient labor politician, was Chairman of the Board of Commissioners of the Port of Oakland and publisher of the *East Bay Labor Journal,* to which he had graduated from a long career as an official of the local Typographical Union. He said, "I have some friends here you should meet," and took me to the next table, where he introduced me as "the man from Washington with the fifteen million dollars for Oakland."

The three at the other table were Dick Groulx, Bob Ash's principal assistant on the staff of the Alameda County Central Labor Council, his wife Pat, and Pete Lee, business agent for the East Bay local of the American Federation of Government Employees. Groulx, an ex-boxer, looked like one still, though overweight, and liked to talk tough and arouse antagonism. Behind the bluster, he was intelligent and realistic, and willing to make reasonable compromises. His wife, a big jolly girl who outweighed him, was full of banter. Pete Lee, a Negro, was aggressive, often abusive, and so committed to the labor union point of view that he defended it against all criticism from Negro spokesmen. His own union had many more Negroes in its membership than most others, which may have blinded him to the barriers existing elsewhere.

I moved my plate over to their table, and we talked until midnight of the labor movement, of what it was doing to help Minorities find employment, and of Oakland. Later we were joined by Russell Crowell, head of the laundry and dry cleaners union, and president of the Labor Council, and a half-dozen other labor officials stopped at our table from time to time and joined in our discussion. One of them was an official of the teamsters' union, who looked the part, with a broken nose and a fighter's stance. Pat Groulx said to him, "It's sure great to have you guys out of the Labor Council. Now anyone can start an argument there without worrying about ending up in the Bay in cement overshoes."

As we talked, I identified myself as a former negotiator of union contracts on the management side and the spokesman

57

for all the New York newspapers during the long strike in 1963. I then discovered something that surprised me and which proved to be a great help in all my future dealings with the strong labor movement in the Bay Area. The fact that I had been in the battle, even though on the other side, formed a strong bond between us. We could discuss past and present labor troubles, speaking the same language, in a way no outsider could, much as generals who have fought on opposite sides are said to be able to talk over old campaigns.

In general, they expressed strong support for opening up all trades to Negroes and much concern for the negative attitudes of the building trades unions about this. They told me that the State Employment Service, in discussions the week before about clearing jobs for training at the Skills Center, had misunderstood their position. They had intended to indicate support for a long list of jobs, including those in the jurisdiction of the building trades. As to the latter, they had said there would be trouble, which would have to be faced in the future, and had been prepared to face a fight with the building trades unions on this issue. The Employment Service, however, had interpreted their statement as opposition and had dropped the building trades categories. They questioned the Employment Service's figures on the need for workers in some categories, but were solid in their support for opening opportunities to Minorities. They said that the two large unions not in the Central Labor Council, the teamsters and the longshoremen, had good records, but warned that the building trades unions would be difficult to handle. Since the other unions would be reluctant to oppose them openly, they regretted that this issue had been eliminated by the Employment Service from the Skills Center, where they would have had an opportunity to handle it quietly behind the scenes.

Since one of the key elements of the EDA program was establishing a research and planning staff in Oakland to guide future decisions about its economic development, I started to explore ways of doing this, both with an independent consulting firm and with members of the Berkeley faculty. The firm was the Social Science Research and Development Corporation of Berkeley, headed by Floyd Hunter, a balding, bland-faced, sharp-eyed former professor of sociology, who had made his mark in this field with his book, *Community Power Structure*. Gene Foley had read it and called Hunter about the possibility of doing research for EDA. He was invited to the Dunsmuir House conference, where Foley asked him to prepare a proposal for evaluating the Oakland project and for setting up an independent research and planning staff to be attached to it. I spent two long evenings with him and his assistant, Norman Rae, reviewing his project and discussing all of Oakland's problems. They had just completed an extensive housing study for the City of Oakland and were very helpful about personalities and issues. As I left on the first evening, Hunter startled me by saying gravely, "The success or failure of your efforts in the next two weeks may well be crucial to the future of all our cities."

At Berkeley, I went to see Dean Joseph Lohman, of the Department of Criminology, who had been recommended by several of the EDA staff as one who knew a lot about Minority problems, and who had followed developments in Oakland very closely. He was enthusiastic about the EDA program and assembled for a luncheon meeting an impressive group of professors from the departments of Economics, Public Health, Sociology, Education, City and Regional Planning, Physics, Law, and Environmental Design. When I had previously suggested including some Berkeley faculty members on a committee to oversee the EDA program, the Oakland businessmen turned the idea down on the ground that they did not need help from "impractical intellectuals with wild ideas." In fact, at this meeting, and in subsequent talks with members of this group, I received many hard-headed, practical suggestions, much closer to Oakland's needs than many that came from business

59

groups. Much needs to be done to bridge the gap that exists between the talent available in the universities on urban questions and the public officials and businessmen dealing with urban problems who could benefit from using it.

The discussion at this luncheon covered a broad range. There was general agreement that EDA should support a new research and planning staff, which should concentrate on finding ways to bring the hard-core unemployed into the training program and selecting the kinds of industry which should be located in Oakland. Up to then, the Berkeley faculty had been called in only to comment on projects already initiated for Oakland, and they felt that they could be more useful if they were asked to help in creating new approaches.

Their suggestions included: exploring new sources of employment, in BART, Medicare, and other Federal programs; getting employers to redesign jobs, as the automobile companies had done in Detroit, to provide opportunities for those with limited skills; revising employment tests on a realistic basis to eliminate unnecessary requirements; and a survey of the skills of the unemployed. An idea that had a direct bearing on my most immediate problem came from Professor Heyman of the Law School: "Can't you make it a prerequisite of a business loan that the borrower employ graduates of the Skills Center?"

The main thrust of my inquiry in these two weeks was to ascertain how we could select a committee which would reflect all points of view in Oakland to make sure that the EDA investment would provide employment for the hard-core unemployed. Since the involvement of the business leadership in this effort was obviously essential to its success, I spent much of my time in exploring their reactions.

My first call was on William F. Knowland, former United States Senator, publisher of the *Oakland Tribune,* whom I had met before at newspaper gatherings. He was locally regarded, as his father had been before him, as the central figure in the

60

Oakland "power structure." Whether or not this was true, he looked the part, with his strong, heavily jowled face, powerful body, and booming voice. Knowing of his conservative views on Federal spending, I expected opposition and hostility when I outlined the EDA program. Instead, he listened with interest and, while he did not commit himself in detail, offered assistance in general terms. His newspaper had published a week before a large section on economic development for Oakland, in which he said in his signed introduction:

Unemployment is at the root of much of the racial unrest. Many of the problems will be solved when jobs are available to the minorities. This time will come after they have acquired skills for the jobs, and that means education. Ultimately, education is the answer. Perhaps a closer liaison between the educators and the industrialists should be sought to determine what it takes to train people properly for the jobs.

One could not ask for a better statement of a large part of the philosophy underlying the EDA program. As it unfolded, Senator Knowland later provided strong support.

I learned most of what I needed to know about business attitudes from two others. One was Ken Thompson, who at the Dunsmuir House meeting had attracted our attention by coming up with a bold, imaginative plan for a public corporation to underwrite a $30 million development program, using all the resources of EDA, to create three thousand new jobs. He was a partner in the nationwide accounting firm of Lybrand, Ross Bros. & Montgomery, into which he had merged his own local firm. He had lived all his life in Oakland and believed in its future. His trained, keen intelligence made him see its problems clearly, but his disarming, almost boyish, enthusiasm kept him from being discouraged at what he saw. While he was active in Republican politics, his approach to Oakland's needs was non-political, highly realistic, and imaginative. Several years earlier, he was one of a small group of

White businessmen who initiated a series of regular meetings with Negro leaders, to see what could be done to accommodate more successfully the rapid increase in the Negro population and to help solve its severe unemployment problems. This led directly to the formation of the Adult Minority Employment Project and laid a solid foundation for the Ford Foundation projects and the Poverty Program community action program.

Thompson filled me in on the history of the two organizations responsible for developing business expansion with Federal loans from the program preceding EDA. One, the Industrial Development Commission, had been set up by Mayor Houlihan as part of the city government, with an annual budget of $100,000. It had conducted a countrywide promotion campaign to bring new business to Oakland, but had produced little in the way of concrete results. The other was the Oakland Economic Development Foundation, formed by the Chamber of Commerce to provide the local financing, 10 percent then and 5 percent under EDA, required as a condition of government loans, long-term and at low interest, for 65 percent of the cost of land, building and equipment for businesses providing new employment in areas of low employment. He arranged for me to meet with the board of the Foundation. This group consisted mainly of the Oakland managers of large utilities and banks, who had little feel for the problems of expanding small businesses and new ventures. They were unhappy about participating in government loans which would give one firm a competitive advantage over another and rejected several applications on this ground by interpreting a clause in the statute more narrowly than the EDA staff thought justified. In general, they seemed to feel that anyone who applied for a government loan because he could not get financing through commercial channels was a bad risk. The Foundation had no staff and had not developed a good working relationship with the Industrial Development Commission, which could have acted as its staff. The result, with which no one was satisfied, was that only eight applications for loans had been received in two years, and of these only two had been approved.

While everyone agreed that something needed to be done, it took a long time to straighten all this out. The problem was one of leadership, which could not be developed in the business community at that time.

The other individual in the business community who helped me a great deal was Norman Nicholson, the Kaiser corporation's vice president for community relations. Kaiser had recently completed a gleaming new headquarters building in Oakland which towered over the rest of the city. It was the largest enterprise headquartered there and had two vice presidents who played a major role in community affairs. One, Nils Eklund, had been at the Dunsmuir House conference and served as Kaiser's representative on the Chamber of Commerce, the Economic Development Foundation, and other business groups. He was out of town during my first weeks in Oakland, but generously loaned me his office and later helped with many aspects of our program. The other, Nicholson, represented Kaiser in all community activities involving Minority groups and Labor. He was vice chairman of the Poverty Council and chairman of the Adult Minority Project.

Of all the people I talked to in my first weeks in Oakland, Nicholson came closest to having a full understanding of the whole community. He showed a strong sympathy and understanding for the problems of other groups, combined with a hard-headed realism about what could be done to solve them, and a readiness to try unorthodox solutions. From him, I learned in detail of the troubles then being experienced by the Poverty Council and the Adult Minority Project. Each of these was then approaching a stalemate, which was worsened by the erratic leadership of Mayor Houlihan, unable to cope with the warring factions within the Minority groups, the sensitivities of the labor unions, and the failure of initiative on the part of business. Being a man of action, and highly sensitive to the urgency of Oakland's situation, Nicholson was in a state of frustration which limited his effectiveness as an operator, but increased it as a source of information.

In the last of several long conversations with him, I summed up my own conclusions from my first two weeks of investigation:

—In the community action program, the Target Area committees were beginning to provide effective participation for ghetto residents, but this needed to be improved. The Poverty Council was operating fairly well in its role of decision making on poverty projects, but it was not the body to become involved in overseeing the EDA program.

—The Adult Minority Employment Project, in difficulty because labor was threatening to pull out of it, was the logical group to act as the advisory committee for the Skills Center, to which its work of recruiting and placing the unemployed was closely linked.

—While much needed to be done to improve the EDA business loan program and the local agencies related to it, this was of less immediate concern than other problems.

—It was hard to see how an effective top-level committee to oversee the EDA program could be formed in a community so divided against itself. If Edgar Kaiser could be persuaded to head such a committee, in time it might provide new leadership, but it seemed unlikely that he would be able to take time from his other responsibilities for this.

In these first two weeks, I met several times with Ben Nutter, executive director of the Port of Oakland and his assistant, Monroe Sullivan, to study the projects submitted by the Port, which offered the principal opportunity for EDA to invest in facilities to create new employment in Oakland. These were: a $10 million hangar at the airport to be leased by the rapidly expanding World Airways; a new marine terminal with access

64

roads, costing $10 million; and a $2 million expansion of the industrial park on land near the airport. Nutter, an engineer, was cautious, slow to make decisions, and rather overwhelmed by the size of this new program, which would nearly double the value of the Port's facilities. Sullivan, more of a promoter and expediter, was a great help in keeping things moving. After we had reviewed these projects, they asked if each would be considered on its own, or as part of a total Oakland package. I said that each would be considered on its own merits, but only after we had worked out an administrative arrangement to ensure that the new jobs created would go to the local unemployed to the fullest extent possible.

In the second week, in the course of a talk with Ken Robertson, Labor Department representative in San Francisco, I learned that his department was about to announce approval of the Skills Center. I knew that this was premature, as EDA had not yet agreed on the amount it would contribute, no advisory committee had been chosen, and not enough jobs had yet been cleared for training. All of these questions would be decided more promptly if government funds were not committed ahead of time. Urgent as the need for the Skills Center was, a few weeks' delay now would avoid much trouble and delay later on. I reported this quickly to Anne Gould, who reacted with anger. She had been the one who had first proposed the Skills Center to Labor and Health, Education, and Welfare and had worked closely with them in setting it up. EDA had offered to provide funds for half its cost, on condition that it have a broadly representative advisory committee, high-quality short-term training, enough jobs cleared for training, and mechanics for ensuring the entry of the hard-core unemployed into the program. None of these conditions had been met, and she had not even been informed of the announcement. She tried to get it held up, but failed.

During this period, I met several times with Jerry Keithley, the City Manager, in Oakland's ornate, well-kept City Hall.

He had been in office only three weeks and seemed somewhat overwhelmed by the complexity of Oakland's administrative and financial problems. Its real-estate tax rate was one of the highest in the state, and could not be increased without a danger of driving more businesses and well-to-do residents out to adjoining communities where the rates were lower. At the same time, Oakland's expenses for police, welfare, education, and other services were increased by the high proportion of unemployed Negroes, who could not obtain housing in the neighboring communities even if they found jobs there. Since Oakland had a strong tradition of operating on a "pay-as-you-go" basis, it was impossible to get voter approval for bond issues for such needed capital improvements as sewers, street lights, paving and curbs, particularly in the ghetto areas.

Keithley explained that, under the Oakland charter, the City Manager was the full-time operating executive, to whom all the City departments reported. He reported to the City Council, not to the Mayor, whose job was a part-time one, presiding over Council meetings and representing the City at various functions. At one time the Mayor had been elected by the Council from among its members, but several years earlier the Charter had been amended to provide for direct election by the voters, and since then the position had acquired more political and popular significance. In practice, the relationship between the Mayor and the City Manager depended very much on the personalities involved. As he told me this, I could see that Keithley, a quiet, unassuming man, might have some trouble working this out with the flamboyant Houlihan.

With Keithley and his department heads, I reviewed all of the projects which they were considering for submission to EDA. Most of these, highway improvements, sewers and street lighting, making Dunsmuir House into a large conference center, had too little relation to the creation of long-term employment to be of interest to EDA, but the access roads to employment areas at the Port's Marine Terminal and the new coliseum and stadium complex seemed possibilities.

My last interview before I returned to Washington was with Mayor Houlihan, on Friday, February 11. When I entered his office, on a bright, sunny California afternoon, he rose and drew the heavy drapes, shutting out the light and the view of his city, leaving us only the electric light on his large desk. His face flushed as he launched into an angry tirade against the "Federal Hawkshaws" and "the new bureaucracy," and referred scornfully to Anne Gould and Andy Bennett. When I tried to interrupt to come to their defense, he said, "Just a minute, let me finish," and went on for forty-five minutes without pausing, emphasizing these main points:

—In a talk with Gene Foley the week before in Washington, he had been disappointed at Foley's continuing insistence that economic development be tied to jobs for the long-term unemployed.

—He was disappointed at the small amounts of money being offered by the new Department of Housing and Urban Development in relation to the total urban problem and emphasized the danger of raising false hopes.

—He was tired of attacks like the one which had just appeared in *The Wall Street Journal*—based on interviews with Curtis Baker and Mark Comfort—written by people who talked only to the "noise makers."

—"Oakland just wants to be left alone."

—He still hoped to work something out with EDA, but was skeptical about this. He thought Foley was sincere, but wished he would not overemphasize employment in connection with development.

When at last I was able to reply, I said I was glad to hear his last statement, since if he had meant what he said earlier about wanting to be left alone, my task was simple. I would be in Washington the next week and could recommend just

67

that. He replied quickly that he did not want to be left alone by EDA, but just by critics like *The Wall Street Journal.*

I told him briefly about my activities in Oakland, and that I was not yet ready to reach a conclusion about the overall structure needed for the EDA program. The statute required that EDA expenditures be devoted to solving the unemployment problem, and we would continue to emphasize this. I concluded: "This may or may not be the best way to solve urban problems, but it is the only way available to EDA. If it works, this will be good for Oakland, and usable elsewhere. If it fails, we will learn from this experience, as EDA did from ARA."

In the course of this talk, Mayor Houlihan indicated that he was thinking of quitting before the end of his term, to make a better living elsewhere. I did not try to dissuade him.

This talk with Houlihan lingered in my mind, when I stopped at my home in Aspen on the way to make my report in Washington. It had a strange quality of unreality. It did not fit in with the other pieces of the Oakland puzzle. I told some friends about it at dinner. One of them shivered, and said, "Be careful; there's something wrong with that man."

On the next Tuesday, February 15, at the end of a long session in Washington with the EDA Oakland group, a call came in from Bill Clayton, EDA field representative in California, asking: "Have you heard about Mayor Houlihan?"

I replied: "No. What has he done?"

"He's resigned, that's what he's done," said Clayton, breathless, "and probably something much worse. It's all over the papers here. Two stories, big headlines. In one, Mayor Houlihan resigns, effective April 30. Here's what he said." He read me excerpts from a long rambling letter from Houlihan to the City Council, covering all the accomplishments of his regime, which ended by explaining that he was resigning because he could not afford to continue in office at the small salary it provided.

"Now listen to this," Clayton went on. "The other story is about an estate which Houlihan, as a lawyer, has been administering for many years. Yesterday, the beneficiary of the estate, an elderly widow, filed a claim for an accounting. In the papers filed in court, her lawyers allege that Houlihan has embezzled over $90,000. That was yesterday afternoon. Houlihan resigned this morning. You draw your own conclusions."

When I repeated this to the group around my desk in Washington, they sat silent, stunned with surprise. Anne Gould was the first to speak: "You were the last one to see him before this happened. You'll be a hero in the ghetto. They'll think you forced him out. Come clean. What didn't you tell us?"

We called Foley to tell him. He too was speechless, just saying, "I'll be damned. What do you think of that."

Frankly, I didn't think much of it. Houlihan, difficult as he had been, was a known quantity. We had felt we could work with him. Now, Oakland would have to choose a new Mayor, an unknown factor capable of tipping the delicate balance of the divided community toward success or failure.

Chapter IV

The New Employment Plan

In WASHINGTON on February 15, before we had heard the news of Houlihan's resignation, I met with all of the EDA team who had been at the Dunsmuir House conference, to review what I had learned there since they left.

In my report to them, I said I had never seen a community so divided within and between each of its parts as Oakland appeared to be. Neither business, labor, minorities, or government contained outstanding individuals who were recognized as spokesmen for the whole group. Such leadership as there was within each group was misinformed about the attitudes and motives of those in the other groups, and each blamed the others for their troubles.

In view of this fragmented leadership, I had concluded that it would be difficult, if not impossible, to create a strong local committee, as we had planned. For the same reason, however, positive action taken by EDA could be effective because there would be little organized opposition. Therefore, I recommended that we proceed project by project to develop a sensible program, postponing for the time being any decision about a top-level committee.

Just as we had finished discussing this and had agreed to

go ahead on this basis, Bill Clayton's call came in from California, telling us of Mayor Houlihan's resignation. After we had reflected on this new uncertainty for a day, we found that it reinforced our determination to waste no time and to go ahead with the projects, in the hope of completing their review by the beginning of April.

Foley approved this plan, and I returned to Oakland. I knew that in just six weeks, we had to complete work on a complex list of projects totaling over $30 million, and before we finished work on them, we had to find a way to tie these projects tightly to local employment.

In Oakland, much of the talk centered on Mayor Houlihan's resignation. Since it was to be effective April 30, he continued in office, but spent most of his time attending meetings out of town and was not available for questioning. On the few occasions when reporters were able to intercept him at the airport—with full local TV coverage—he pushed angrily through them, muttering, "No comment—I can account for everything —no comment." His lawyers asked for repeated postponements in the estate proceeding, until the court finally ordered him to appear in April.

Many who thought he had been a good mayor were amazed and puzzled, unable to explain the close timing of the suit against him and his resignation. Even his enemies hesitated to believe that he was stupid enough to be caught stealing in this way.

Under the City Charter, the City Council was responsible for electing his successor, to serve until the next general election a year later. It seemed likely that the conservative majority on the Council would elect one of their number, an unhappy prospect, since in the view of most local observers, their conservatism was exceeded only by their stupidity.

In the ghetto, where many enjoyed the thought that Houlihan had been caught stealing, the feeling was universal that, even if found guilty, he would never go to jail for it. "He's not like one of us, who get jailed even for what we didn't do. He's in the power structure, and they will save him. You'll see."

Dick Daschbach soon joined me in Oakland to begin to interview the large number of applicants for business loans, who had been attracted by the publicity about the Dunsmuir House meeting, and to try to revitalize the local machinery for participating in these loans. Andy Bennett came to work out with Floyd Hunter a proposal for setting up a research and planning staff. To make a preliminary review of the big public works projects of the Port and the City and to work on the problems of the Skills Center, I brought both Blair Butterworth and Doug Costle. By then we had found two sparsely furnished offices in the Federal building across from City Hall and a good secretary. It was a busy place.

Toward the end of February, while the others were going ahead with these projects, my main concern continued to be the search for a way to tie the projects to jobs for Oakland's unemployed. Soon after I came back from Washington, I had a sharp reminder of the need to produce something specific on this. On the Washington's Birthday holiday, we had no telephone service in the Federal building where we had a temporary office. After trying all day to reach me, John Frykman, who was very agitated, finally called in the evening at my motel to tell me about a meeting that morning of an "ad hoc committee" of Negro and White ministers, at which there was much resentment over the lack of consultation about the EDA program. They had heard that seven Port projects and three business loans were already being considered in Washington. Unable to reach me, they had checked with the EDA field representative for the area, who had not been at Dunsmuir House. He told them that "there were no EDA regulations that required the recipient of a grant or loan to employ the long-term unemployed, and that instead it was just expected that the jobs created would eventually result in such employment."

I told Frykman that this had been the approach in the past, but that we were trying something new in Oakland and would find a way to link the jobs more closely to the local unemployed. He urged that ghetto representatives be involved at an earlier stage in the approval of projects. He refused to tell me more about the ad hoc committee or what it planned to do, but the implication was clear. Suspecting that EDA, like BART, might make commitments that failed to guarantee jobs for the unemployed in the ghetto, they were considering protest demonstrations. The three weeks that had passed since the Dunsmuir House announcement did not seem to me like much time to reach a reassuring decision, but it seemed too long to them.

Thinking about the projects we were reviewing, I was impressed by the wide variety of employment needs involved. A business loan to a bakery or to a car wash would provide a small number of jobs requiring limited skills, which could be taught on the job. The big hangar for World Airways would open up nearly one thousand jobs for aircraft mechanics, for whom complex training courses would be needed, lasting thirty months, to meet CAB licensing requirements. Each employer who was able to expand his business in Oakland because of the EDA investment there would have a different mix of job requirements.

The extent to which these jobs would be filled by recruiting and training residents of Oakland would depend on decisions to be made by each employer. Our first thought had been that all such employers could be influenced by a high-level committee which would establish and enforce employment standards. After deciding that it would not be possible to form such a committee in Oakland at that time, I began to realize that a nonspecific attempt to apply a general standard of "maximum possible employment" of ghetto residents was not satisfactory; it would be interpreted differently by everyone concerned and would be hard to enforce after employment decisions had been made.

Having been an employer myself, on a large newspaper, I thought we might get much better results if we asked each employer to tell us what he could do affirmatively to provide employment for the hard-core unemployed, and what training would be required. If we approved the employer's plan, it could become part of the agreement between us. If his plan did not provide enough employment, he would not become eligible for a loan or lease financed by EDA.

I tried this idea out on the EDA staff who were then in Oakland, suggesting that a simple, easy approach would be to include in all loan agreements and leases a requirement that the employer follow his employment plan as previously approved by EDA. This could be submitted to a special local committee, with ample Minority and Target Area representation, for review and approval before the loan or lease was completed. Most of them liked the idea, though some felt that EDA would be reluctant to get so deeply involved in each employer's continuing operations.

I then wrote out a short, two-page explanation, headed "Employment Plans and Review." It required each employer to submit an Employment Plan, to be approved by an Employment Review Board before EDA would approve his lease or loan. The Board would include representatives of business, labor, EDA, and each of the Target Areas, the latter being in the majority. Monthly reports on hiring would be filed. Noncompliance with the Plan would be a condition of default in the lease or loan. I was convinced, as I said at the time, that this would "cut through our toughest Gordian knot, which we'll never unravel otherwise." I knew that, because it was new and had not been tried before, much persuasion would be needed to sell it to everyone involved. During the next week I discussed it with Frykman and others close to the ghetto, with labor, and with employers, including Ed Daly of World Airways, whose employment plan would cover nearly a thousand jobs. All favored it as a direct, practical solution.

Warnings about difficulties in applying it came from two quite different sources. The first was from my secretary, Carol Bradley. A Negro, she had grown up in nearby Richmond in a ghetto much like the Oakland Flatlands. While I was dictating a letter to Foley about the Employment Plan, she looked up with a worried expression. I asked, "Is anything the matter?" With a shy smile, she leaned forward and said:

"Yes. I think it's wonderful what you guys are trying to do here, but I'm afraid it's just not going to work. I live with the kind of people you are talking about—the unemployed, who need training. There are about ten percent of us who are highly motivated, and who will get training and jobs even if the government doesn't help. There are another ten to fifteen percent, probably no more than in any other group of people, who are against everything, who you will never reach.

"It is the ones in between that I'm not sure about. At the beginning, the Skills Center will be the big thing, and a lot of them will sign up. But training will turn out to be hard work and take a long time. After the newness wears off, and they are getting a little discouraged, they'll run into some of the bad ones in the bar or the pool room, who'll say, 'What's the point in that training stuff? Why do that, man, when you could be having a good time here with us, and getting dinner from Susie one night, and Mary the next, and all like that?' A lot of them will drop out then, unless you can find some way to get them motivated from the top instead of the bottom.

"I can see this in my own family. My mother had a civil service job. My father left when we were young. She brought my sister and me up to want good jobs and to do well in school so we could get them. My stepfather doesn't care about this. My stepbrothers are a problem, because they want more than they can get. They look at you, Whitey, sitting in a white

75

shirt behind your big desk and say, 'That's what I want to do.' But they don't stop to think how much schooling and hard work at smaller jobs it took you to get there, and they're not going to be satisfied with the jobs you can give them."

I asked her why she had not gone on to college. She said, "We needed another pay check at home. I knew I could be a good secretary and would like it. I wasn't so sure I'd be happy in college. Now I'm glad I didn't go on. I'm having a much better time in this busy, crazy place working with all you guys than I would studying a lot of strange subjects."

The next morning she came in and said, "Last night I was talking to my mother about what I said to you. She brought up something else I forgot. You're going to have to do something about welfare to get a lot of people interested in training and jobs. For many, they are better off with welfare payments than they will be when they are taking training and sometimes than when they finally get jobs. That is certainly so for young mothers my age with babies at home, who need to pay for babysitting and better clothes if they leave home for training and a job."

I told her that I was sure she was right on both points, but that we had to move one step at a time. The first step was to provide the jobs and the training. We could then figure out how to remove the obstacles to getting people through the training and into the jobs.

The second warning came later from the same Berkeley faculty group I had met in February. They liked the concept of the Employment Plan, but expressed grave doubts about the government's ability to administer it successfully, by providing adequate staff to work with each employer to develop plans that would really reach the hard-core unemployed. If this were not done, they feared that the EDA program would just be another source of frustration and disappointment in the ghetto.

As soon as I was sure that the Employment Plan idea would

be acceptable to those most concerned in Oakland, I sent it off to Foley to get his reaction. He called on March 9, to say that he liked it, and that he would take it up promptly with the EDA legal department. Doug Costle, who had returned to Washington to expedite the processing of the Oakland projects there, called the next week to report that the EDA legal staff had raised some serious objections, most of which seemed to grow out of their hesitancy to get involved in new and untried contractual arrangements.

This was the beginning of a long battle in Washington, which, from Oakland, I found hard to understand. In all my discussions locally, with employers, labor officials, and Minority and ghetto representatives, the Employment Plan was accepted as a realistic, practical solution. In Washington, however, many of those in the EDA legal, business loan, and public works divisions who had not studied the Oakland situation on the spot regarded it with suspicion as an unnecessary complication. It caused them much administrative discomfort and met with strong resistance.

During the last week of March, after hearing the questions raised by counsel and by others, Foley approved the Employment Plan procedure as an integral part of the Oakland experiment and directed his staff to make it part of the nationwide EDA program.

This Employment Plan Review system had two new features which distinguished it from all previous attempts to secure employment for Negroes and others barred by discrimination or lack of training. One was the direct, contractual commitment by each employer, tied in with available training programs, to place them in specific jobs. Employers liked this, and it worked well, because it provided a clear, understandable agreement tailored to the needs of each business.

The other innovation was the direct participation of ghetto residents, designated as members of the Employment Plan Review Board by their Target Area committees, in the initial ap-

77

proval of each employer's Plan and in the monthly review of his performance under it. The Review Board had seven members, representing labor, management, EDA, and each of the four Target Areas. This gave the Target Areas, speaking for the unemployed, a clear majority. Its role was advisory, since EDA, as the government agency responsible for committing its funds, retained the final right to approve or disapprove each plan. This, too, worked well in practice. It gave the Target Area representatives an effective voice in deciding whether each EDA project was designed to provide maximum employment in the ghetto. In its meetings, the different members of the Review Board exchanged information and reached decisions on a realistic, rather than a partisan, basis.

The idea of majority representation for the Target Areas on the Review Board—which did much to establish the credibility and good faith of the EDA program in the ghetto— evolved from our observation of the Oakland Poverty Program Council and Target Area committees during February, as they struggled to resolve the statutory requirement of maximum feasible representation of the poor on the Council. At that time, similar community action councils all over the country were debating the question of what this meant, since it had to be reduced to numbers on each committee. The statutory language was vague, and the interpretations issued by the Office of Economic Opportunity did little to clarify it, so each council had to reach its own decision.

In many cases, the business, labor, and middle-class Minority members of the committees had had little contact with the realistic, articulate ghetto residents who had much to offer to these committees. They knew the poor mainly through their most militant and aggressive spokesmen. As a result, they feared that a large representation of the poor would disrupt their meetings and fill the committee with people who lacked practical experience and judgment. Ghetto residents, on the other hand, knew well that they knew more about their problems and what they needed. They felt that they should have a majority on the committee, so that they could control its actions.

The question of 51 percent representation had been raised at the regular monthly meeting of the Poverty Council in January, before we started the EDA program. Judge Wilson, its chairman, was opposed to changing its membership and quickly cut off debate. This had caused much resentment in the Target Area committees, who prepared to make it a major issue at the next meeting.

This was held on February 23, in the gymnasium of Lazear High School. A long table had been set up in the center of the floor, for the forty members of the Poverty Council; almost all of them attended. Folding chairs several rows deep around all four sides were filled with spectators, most of them Negroes from Oakland. An efficient public address system was provided, with microphones in front of each committee member and four others out on the floor for members of the audience to use when recognized by the Chairman.

All of the EDA group then in Oakland, Bennett, Butterworth, Costle, and Daschbach, went to this meeting, which lasted from 8 p.m. until after midnight. When we entered, I said hello to Curtis Baker, who this time was wearing a blazing red shirt with matching socks. He refused to shake hands with me, saying loudly, for the benefit of those around him, "I won't have nothing to do with you, 'cause you been dealing with Houlihan."

Norm Nicholson, of Kaiser, vice chairman of the Poverty Council, chaired this meeting, since Judge Wilson did not attend. Throughout the long, stormy session he managed, with skill, patience, and humor, to give everyone a chance to talk, but also to keep the discussion on the track, and to get a decision on each item on the long agenda. Members of the Poverty Council spoke first, and then comments and questions

79

were permitted from the audience—a useful device for getting community reactions and letting off steam.

Members from the North Oakland and Fruitvale Target Areas opened the meeting by reading letters criticizing Judge Wilson, as chairman at the January meeting, for cutting off discussion on the question of maximum feasible participation of the poor, while expressing his own views freely.

The proponents of 51 percent representation had prepared themselves well for this meeting. The first point was the election to the Poverty Council of the Reverend Alexander Jackson, Negro minister, and Dick Groulx, of the Labor Council staff, who had been nominated to fill vacancies. The Target Area members opposed them, declaring that all vacancies should be filled by Target Area representatives until the figure of 51 percent was reached. The opposition failed, and the two were elected by a large majority, including many Target Area members.

The Target Area group then offered a motion that the principle of 51 percent representation for the Target Areas be approved and that a way be found to achieve this as soon as possible. This was discussed for an hour. The concept received strong support from Clinton White, a young and successful trial lawyer, a Negro, and president of the NAACP. This was the third time in a month that I had heard him take a strong stand for the Negroes in the poverty area, once at the meeting on BART employment, and again at a lunch for a Negro business group, when he had advocated militant, direct action to overcome labor union resistance to opening jobs to Negroes. Along with Don McCullum and Carl Metoyer, two other Negro lawyers on the Poverty Council, he was at this time moving in to provide strong Negro leadership in a more militant way than had been done by middle-class Negroes before Watts. While questions were raised by some of the labor and business members, there was no strong opposition, and the motion passed with a good majority.

The next three hours were devoted to the approval of a long list of projects. One, for support of the Good Samaritan Home greatly pleased Joan Sparks until the Poverty Program staff told her she would have to resign from the Poverty Council if it was approved in Washington, a rule which several members protested.

The last item to come up was the report of a subcommittee recommending that the Poverty Council set up a Police Review Board, to hear complaints against the police. It would be set up outside the city government, with no subpoena or disciplinary powers, and financed by the Ford Foundation, as the Poverty Program lacked the authority. This motion had the enthusiastic support of all Minority spokesmen. Although some of the business members spoke against it, it passed, at 12:45 a.m., with a large majority.

Early in the meeting, all of the EDA staff had been introduced. As we left, Curtis Baker stopped us to say, "How come there are no Black faces in your group? Doesn't that Commerce Department back there have any Black men to send out to us?" By chance, not design, when I left Oakland eight months later, four of the five members of the EDA staff remaining there were Negroes.

The February meeting was the first time that any of the EDA staff had been to a Poverty Program community action committee meeting. Each of us was favorably impressed. We had all been skeptical about much of the Poverty Program, which we felt had tried to do too much too fast, without getting at the main poverty need—employment. Also, its failures had been more widely reported than its successes. The process of involving the Target Area committee representatives seemed successful. We all felt that the establishment of this communication and involvement justified the program, quite apart from the value of individual projects.

A week later, Walt Miller, the new head of the Skills Center, and I went to an evening meeting of the Fruitvale Target Area committee to describe our programs. We finished about 9 p.m., and from then until midnight listened to the committee debate about the way in which their committee should be represented on the Poverty Council. They assumed that each Target Area's delegation would be increased from five to eight, giving the four areas thirty-two members on a council of sixty. The question being discussed was whether a majority, five, or up to seven, of the delegation should be poor people, whose incomes were at the poverty level defined in the statute. A wide diversity of views appeared:

—"No one can really speak for the poor who is not poor himself."

—"Only a Negro can really understand the problems of Negroes."

—"What I wants is that maximum feas . . . whatever it is I wants more of it."

—"Once we have fifty-one percent on the committee, what we need to represent us are those who can speak best for us, whether or not they are poor or Negroes."

—"We need a Mexican-American on the committee, and it doesn't matter if he is poor, so long as he understands our problems, which are different from those of Negroes or Anglos."

In this discussion, it was apparent that local reactions to the strong influence of the White ministers of the East Oakland Parish, who had played a leading role in the argument for 51 percent representation, were factors on both sides. Some of the local residents wanted to make sure that these ministers continued on the delegation, while others wanted to give the poor a larger role, less under their dominant leadership. The ministers themselves, who took part in the debate, were divided. Some obviously felt that the poor were now ready to take greater responsibility. Others were less sure and thought it was too soon for the White leaders to step aside.

The final decision was that the delegation should contain a

majority of poor people, and that one member of the delegation should be a Mexican-American.

In talking about these meetings, all of us in the EDA group agreed that the action on the Police Review Board and on 51 percent representation had been significant victories, which had done much to relieve tensions in the ghetto by convincing its residents that they could act to influence important decisions affecting their lives. This reinforced our conclusion, in creating the Employment Plan Review Board that a majority of its members should be designated by the Target Areas, to provide it with a strong voice speaking for the unemployed, who, after all, were the reason for EDA's investment in Oakland.

When it became evident that the new Employment Plan idea could provide the necessary link between the EDA projects and the unemployed, Foley decided to return to Oakland in March for three days of meetings with all elements in the community, to discuss and explain the Employment Plan, the Skills Center, and all EDA projects.

Chapter V

The New Mayor Moves In

At the Dunsmuir House meeting, Foley had said that EDA would act "in partnership with the city," and "in a creative blend with private interest." In this, we knew that the Mayor would be a central figure in the action which would determine the success or failure of our program. Elected by all the citizens of the city, he was in a unique position to maintain effective contact with Minority groups, labor, and business, and to bring them together with the city government to solve their problems. If he had the support of businessmen, he could persuade them to work with EDA in providing employment. His position gave him ready access to publicity in newspapers, radio, and television. He could use these to arouse community support for the program, to explain it, and to call attention to its shortcomings.

Houlihan's abrupt resignation on February 15 left us curious about his successor. We wondered how helpful he would be and when we could start working with him. Two weeks later, the City Council elected one of its members, John Reading, to be the new Mayor.

I went to see him as soon as I could, on March 3. We met with Jerry Keithley, the city manager, in his office, where the new Mayor was spending a lot of time learning about the details of city government. A lean, intense man, Reading gave an impression of controlled, strong energy as he talked, turning in his chair, crossing and recrossing his legs, moving his hands for emphasis, gripping the chair arm or table edge so hard that his fingers whitened, and often rubbing his cheek and supporting his chin. I had heard that he had grown up in Oakland, served six years in the Air Force after graduating from Berkeley, and then, after the war, started his own food processing business in Oakland. In twenty years, he had built this from scratch to a profitable group of companies grossing over $1 million a year, with several plants in Mexico and California. He had been appointed to the City Council in 1961 and elected to a four-year term two years later. He was said to be a middle-of-the-road Republican, seriously interested in improving Oakland's government.

He told me that he planned to make a full-time job of being Mayor, since his wife, who had been his business partner, and other executives, could run his companies, which produced ample income for his and his family's needs. Earnestly, he said, "I really care about Oakland and its future, and want to do what I can to make it a better place to live in, for all its people." We talked for over an hour, discussing all the city's problems. I told him how much we had learned by direct experience in the poverty areas and urged him to eliminate the barriers built up in the past between them and City Hall. His response to this was cautious, but he seemed interested. "Oakland's biggest problem today," he said, "is the lack of employment for so many of the Negroes who moved here in such numbers during and after the War. I used to be opposed to big Federal spending on aid programs, but in my five years on the Council, as I have learned what Oakland faces, with the big influx of unskilled Negroes who can't get jobs, and the exodus of well-to-do taxpayers to the suburbs, I have changed my mind. Oakland will never solve its problems without Fed-

85

eral aid, a lot of it, for economic development, for training, for housing, and urban renewal. The Federal government should pay for these, because its policies caused many of our problems. I am worried, though, about whether all this Federal money will be spent wisely and don't want to see it go down the drain or be wasted in any way."

As we talked, I realized that he naturally favored a direct, personal approach. His experience as a small businessman, not part of a big organization, had reinforced this. But unlike many successful, "self-made" men, he did not take the attitude that the unemployed members of Minority groups should also be able to make it on their own. He emphasized that much help was needed to bridge the gap between available jobs and those who lacked the education and experience needed to fill them.

I presented the EDA program in detail, as he had not been at Dunsmuir House. Reading expressed great interest in industrial development, saying he was ready to take a fresh look at the way Oakland had handled this in the past. He was sure there were several hundred small businesses in Oakland, ready to expand if they could get financing, which should be informed of the EDA program. But he was wary about the complexity of Federal procedures and the delays these caused, describing a bad time he had had with the Small Business Administration in his own business some years before.

After I left, I noted in my diary: "Reading is rather cold in manner, and it is hard to tell how he responded on some issues, but this may be partly caution at the beginning of his job."

There was good reason for caution in approaching the turbulent Oakland scene that March. The February Poverty Council victories of the ghetto representatives regarding the Police Review Board and 51 percent representation of the poor had provoked a conservative reaction. After raising hopes for ghetto employment by the Dunsmuir House announcement

86

at the end of January, EDA had been working quietly behind the scenes, but could not yet produce concrete results. The premature announcement of the Skills Center had caused confusion in the ghetto and had increased frictions between Minority groups and the labor unions. Several church groups were considering a proposal to bring Saul Alinsky to help organize the poor in Oakland, a prospect likely to add to the tensions between the ghetto and the establishment.

Toward the middle of March, the Oakland ghetto had begun its own newspaper, *The Flatlands*. Financed by small contributions, it was mainly the work of two girls, Alexandra Close, who wrote most of it and Lynn Phipps, whose striking photographs of ghetto personalities and places added much to its impact. The members of its Editorial Board, which included Curtis Baker and Mark Comfort, were all ghetto residents. Their frequent articles added flavor and vitality. Under its masthead motto, "Tell it like it is and do what is needed," it gave broad coverage to housing, schools, police actions, and everything else of interest in the ghetto. Twice a month until December, when it ran out of money, the ghetto spoke with vigor and eloquence in its eight to twelve tabloid pages. Beside a picture of a real-estate firm's billboard in a muddy dump at the city limit reading, "Welcome to Oakland, The All America City," the first issue of *Flatlands* began:

FLATLANDS SAYS:

Welcome to Oakland, the all-American city; welcome to Oakland, the "city of pain."

380,000 of us people live in this city. Most of the well-to-do whites and a small number of well-to-do Negroes live in the Oakland hills. . . . From their homes they look down onto a patchwork of grey. That's where the flatlands are, stretching out from the base of their hills and running on to the very edge of the bay. The flatlands are spilling over with people. The flatlands stink with decay.

The flatlands people have had no one to speak for them. . . . Let's

87

spell it out for this all-American city, spell it out the way it is—from the poor's point of view. We'll be one-sided but it's a side that's been hidden too long. It's time that it be brought out and listened to. . . .

Seems like Watts made the federal government jumpy. People from Washington, they come all the way down here. They ask us what's going on in the flatlands. They want to know how long we can wait. Some of the national magazines and newspapers write about us too. They say the flatlands is an area in which we have a so-called "potential explosion." But the people that count, they say that isn't true. They sit way back there on their easy chairs; they tell us everything's all right. After all, they say, "we have not only a strong council but a strong city government and a strong chief of police." When something happens, man, they won't know why. How could they? . . .

City government's no mystery to us. City government likes things as they are. Pretty soon there'll be a new mayor and a new police chief. That won't matter. They've run with the pack pretty long. It's like city government's just one big structure; and it won't bend or crack at all. We don't down any one person; we down the whole works, the whole way of thinking and promising and doing nothing. We're not going to take it no more.

Houlihan, still officially the Mayor, was away from Oakland most of March. His lawyers were fighting a delaying action against his appearing in court in the estate proceeding. His absence, and the unfavorable reaction to his tactics, left a dangerous vacuum in City Hall.

Fortunately, John Reading proved to be much less cautious that I had expected.

His first opportunity to move, which he fumbled, came at a meeting of the City Council on Tuesday, March 8. Several of the more conservative members of the Council had called for a report from the Poverty Council to explain the establishment of the Police Review Board. To the surprise of many, Judge Lionel Wilson, its chairman, who appeared to most Negroes and Whites to be a conservative, middle-class Negro, strongly

88

defended the board. He described the action taken in February to seek Ford Foundation support for such a body. After some antagonistic comments from the City Council members opposed to any kind of Police Review Board, Reading cut in to ask whether, in fact, actions of the Poverty Council were subject to review and control by the City Council.

Judge Wilson, on the defensive, asserted strongly that the Poverty Council was an independent body, not subject to the City Council's control, with full authority to approve applications for Poverty Program and Ford Foundation grants. Mayor Houlihan, who was presiding, intervened to say that the Poverty Council had been asked to report "for information only," and adjourned the meeting before any further action could be taken.

Because of its timing, this question from the Mayor-elect was widely interpreted in the ghetto as an indication that he was hostile toward the Poverty Council and its recent actions. Reading reacted in the direct, open manner which was to become one of his principal assets. He appeared at the next Poverty Council meeting, held the following Saturday, March 12, at Dunsmuir House, to make a conciliatory statement at the beginning of the meeting. He explained that the City Council's action in calling for a report had been for information only and was not an attempt to control the Poverty Council's actions. He said that he regarded the Poverty Council as an important positive factor in Oakland, and that as Mayor he would want to work closely with it. His only interest was to make Oakland a better place for all, and he would not oppose any group that was contributing to Oakland's progress.

This Poverty Council meeting had originally been scheduled as a workshop session, to review program and procedures. Word had spread, however, that an attempt would be made to reverse the action taken at the previous meeting to approve 51 percent representation from the Target Areas. As a result, they were well represented in the Council and among the spectators. This gave Reading a good audience for his opening statement. The action which followed provided him with some useful examples of the divisions within Oakland.

Judge Wilson, who was presiding, then reopened the question of 51 percent representation. I had heard, and this was confirmed by his approach, that he regarded the action on this question at the February meeting, coupled with the letters read there protesting the way he had handled it at the January meeting, as a direct attack on his position and record as chairman, engineered by the White ministers and the Negroes who were active in the Target Areas. Judge Wilson, a successful Negro lawyer who had become a judge several years earlier, was a mild and pleasant man in private conversation, but as chairman, he let his habits of the courtroom interfere, and cut off argument that he regarded as irrelevant or unnecessary, and argued with those with whom he disagreed. His own record in the civil rights field was impressive, but since many of those he gaveled down in the Council meetings were the militant younger Negroes, they regarded him as an Uncle Tom.

At this time the four successful Negro lawyers on the Poverty Council—Judge Wilson, Carl Metoyer, Don McCullum, and Clinton White, had been moving toward a more militant position. In recent months, they had traveled far in this direction. An important factor in their motivation was their growing consciousness of their roles as Negroes, which turned them away from their earlier drive for adaptation and integration with the White community and toward an assumption of responsibility for the entire Negro community. Don McCullum, the first time we talked, said, "Look, Brad, we might as well accept the fact that we live in a racist society, and that this fact will affect almost everything we are working on." I told him I would accept this, since he believed it, for our generation, hoping that what we were doing would make it less true in the next. He went on: "In these times, no White man, no matter how dedicated, can really understand the Negro, or speak for

90

him. Only the Negro can do this today. Even the middle-class Negro, though educated with Whites and accepted in White society, can understand the poor Negro better than any White minister living and working with poor Negroes."

In providing new leadership for the ghetto Negroes, they did not displace the White ministers of the parishes, or the indigenous militants like Curtis Baker. Working with them, they superimposed a more sophisticated and experienced form of leadership, reinforced by their ability to deal and negotiate as equals with politicians and labor leaders.

At the February Poverty Council meeting, they had actively supported the resolutions endorsing 51 percent representation for the Target Areas and the Police Review Board. Judge Wilson, who did not attend that meeting, agreed with the others on the Police Review Board, but felt that the 51 percent resolution went too far and apparently persuaded the others to modify their position. In this, he had the support of Norvel Smith and some of the staff of the Department of Human Resources, who feared that a Council controlled by the Target Areas might set policies with which they did not agree, or which would cause difficulties in Washington.

Judge Wilson came to this meeting well prepared. He introduced a resolution, obviously cleared in advance with a majority of the committee, which provided that 51 percent of the Council members should be representatives of Minority organizations (such as the NAACP, the Urban League, and the Mexican-American Political Association) and of the Target Areas. This would have left the Target Areas with a minority of twelve in a Council of forty members, or sixteen out of forty-four, if their representation were increased as previously planned. In support of this motion, Judge Wilson read a long letter from the director of the Poverty Program office in San Francisco on its interpretation of the requirement of maximum feasible representation of the poor, which set one-third as a guide line and urged that all elements in the community be represented. From this he concluded: "Control by any one group would be the opposite of 'community action.' "

The Reverend Brad Bryant, the White minister on the Fruitvale Target Area delegation who had led the February debate for 51 percent representation promptly offered an amendment that the size of the Council be increased to sixty, with an additional five to come from each of the four target areas, giving them a total of thirty-six.

Judge Wilson called for debate on the amendment, going around the Council table, limiting each member to a five-minute statement, and permitting no interventions from the audience. Only the delegates from the Target Areas—except East Oakland—favored the amendment. Don McCullum made a strong statement opposing it, on the ground that Judge Wilson's resolution would give a better balance to the Council and keep it from reaching an unwieldy size. After Brad Bryant and Bob Olmstead, White ministers on the delegations representing Fruitvale and North Oakland, had spoken for the amendment, Carl Metoyer, a Negro lawyer, said pointedly, "I would like to know who these ministers really think *they* represent." The amendment was defeated by a vote of twenty-one to six, and then Judge Wilson's motion was carried by the same vote.

Gerald Leo, chairman of the Fruitvale Target Area committee, a young Chinese-American whose energy and hard work had made his committee the most active and effective of the four, rose in the audience to read a statement. Judge Wilson ruled him out of order, on the ground that he was not a Council member. The Target Area delegates protested. When Judge Wilson held firm, they all—except two from East Oakland—rose and walked out of the meeting.

In the coffee break that followed, Don McCullum joined the Target Area people in a side room and, in a loud, gesticulating negotiation, worked out a compromise proposal that would have permitted them to rejoin the Council. Before the meeting resumed, I watched him go up and explain it to Judge Wilson, who shook his head vigorously, wanting no compromise.

The Council went ahead without the Target Area members, and Judge Wilson appointed a committee to consider the question of maximum feasible participation, with Don McCullum as chairman. The next item on the agenda was "the role of the Target Area committees." On the recommendation of Norvel Smith, head of the Department of Human Resources, the Council voted unanimously against a proposal from the Target Areas that they be given a veto over programs affecting their areas and the right to approve staff assigned to each area, and instead affirmed that the Council was the sole policy-making body, and that the Target Area Committees were only advisory. Then a resolution was adopted which prohibited the Target Area committees from serving as sponsors of programs and required that all changes in the operations and services of the service centers in each Target Area be approved by Dr. Smith or by the Council.

While this burial service was being conducted, the Target Area representatives were acting very much alive. They called a press conference, and converted their statement into a telegram to President Johnson and Sargent Shriver. It requested that the Target Area Committees be recognized jointly as the official Oakland Community Action Program Agency, with its own staff, to replace the Council and the Department of Human Resources. They said, "We have tried in every way possible to represent the concerns of poor people in our communities. In spite of this, the Council has followed its own course, funded agencies that are not trusted by the poor, supported programs that are not wanted by the poor, and in general refused our advice and counsel."

At the end of the Council meeting, Judge Wilson read their full statement. He noted that it was typewritten, saying, "It is pretty clear this had been discussed and set up before they got here." He omitted to add that his own resolution had also been typed up and circulated in advance, with one big difference—he had also rounded up the votes needed to pass it.

This walkout received nationwide publicity. It created the impression in Washington that the Oakland Poverty Program was in serious trouble and caused the program's headquarters to send out an investigating team headed by its Inspector General. I reported to Foley that, in my opinion, "this was not so much of a disaster as the press reports indicated. McCullum's negotiations with the Target Area people may well result in a stronger Council in the end. Basically, the Poverty Program is suffering from the success of its Oakland operation in reaching the Target Areas and in creating neighborhood leadership."

To pursue Reading's expressed interest in the EDA business loan program, Dick Daschbach and I went to see him on March 16. He fired the opening round in what was to be a long campaign, urging EDA to avoid the troubles that Bay Area Rapid Transit was then experiencing on Minority employment, by taking immediate affirmative steps with the building trades unions to make sure that the construction jobs financed with EDA grants and loans were opened up to Minority residents of Oakland. I assured him that we would try to do this.

Reading then said that a recent survey showed one thousand five hundred businesses in metropolitan Oakland with twenty-five or more employees. He was sure that many of the owners would expand if they had more complete knowledge of EDA and other government development programs. He outlined a plan for a series of meetings at which EDA, the Small Business Administration, and the Port of Oakland could describe their programs. We readily agreed.

To fill the vacancy created on the City Council by his election as Mayor, Reading nominated Carl Metoyer, one of the younger Negro lawyers active in both civil rights and in poli-

94

tics in Oakland. Had he been elected, Metoyer would have been far and away the ablest and most articulate member of a Council not noted for either quality, and the second Negro on the nine-member Council, in a city whose population was nearly 40 percent Negro. The conservative majority of the Council were not pleased with this prospect. Instead they nominated and elected a Japanese American, Frank Ogawa, a successful and wealthy businessman, with whom they could be more comfortable and still give representation to a Minority. Though Reading lost this move in the Council, he did win the praise and support of Don McCullum, Clinton White, and other friends of Metoyer in the civil rights field. Their support was tentative, and they remained critical of his position on many issues, but it came at a good time and laid the ground-work for effective future cooperation.

In working with Minority leaders, Reading was realistic, and able to understand that they, also realists, would cooperate with him on issues on which they agreed and oppose him on those where they disagreed, with equal vigor. He never was able to establish this same rapport with labor leaders, at least while I was in Oakland, since he was put off by their more doctrinaire attitude, which was, in effect, "If you're not with us all the way we're against you all the way."

Toward the end of March, Oakland faced a new and di-visive pressure, to bring in Saul Alinsky, a pioneer in organiz-ing community action in the ghettos. Starting with a highly successful project in Chicago in the thirties, he had applied and refined the techniques developed there in many other cities. His approach was abrasive, designed to subject the con-servative power structures of government and business to every possible form of embarrassment and ridicule. A figure of con-troversy, he was regarded by many as a "radical agitator." His technique was to teach ghetto residents how to use their politi-cal and economic power and to expose in the most telling way the selfish attitudes of those who opposed them. For this pur-

95

pose, he trained ghetto residents to act as organizers, so that after a year or two of help from him they could continue on their own. The organization which he headed, in Carmel, Calif., was called the Industrial Areas Foundation. It cost $200,000 or more to retain their services.

Early in 1966, Alinsky had been seeking funds to set up a training center for organizers in San Francisco, believing that his trainees could be far more effective than those being sent out to organize community action by the new Poverty Program, which he held in low esteem. Several Bay Area church groups, when approached about this, were eager to support it if it could be converted into an action program in Oakland. The Oakland Council of Churches called a meeting of several hundred ministers and lay leaders, to discuss this proposal, in the First Presbyterian Church on Friday, April 1.

John Reading felt strongly that he had enough on his hands already, and that Alinsky would simply increase existing hostilities and delay effective solutions. But he realized that a negative position was not enough, so he went to the Council of Churches meeting to present a positive program of his own and spent nearly two hours giving a major speech outlining this program and answering questions. After warning the Council that the Alinsky approach would be likely to increase hate, anger, and divisiveness in the city, he said that his own five-point program was designed to create jobs and to "open up communications between City Hall and the voiceless Minorities." The last was an unfortunate choice of words, which brought the immediate response from some Minority leaders that there was nothing wrong with their voices, deaf ears at City Hall caused the trouble. It soon became apparent that John Reading's ears, at least, were not deaf.

The five-point program which he presented was:

1) Full cooperation with EDA's $15 million job-creation program, with emphasis on maximum hiring of Minorities.

2) Training programs for Target Area leadership.

3) An "open door" at City Hall. He promised to "listen to anyone who wants to come in and talk to me," and to treat all with "respect, dignity, and courtesy," qualities that all knew had frequently been lacking there in the past, not only in dealing with Minorities.

4) A Human Relations Committee of three Councilmen and four Target Area representatives to improve communications between City Hall and the poor, by helping city officials learn at first hand "what people with lower incomes want," and to acquaint the poor with City Hall's problems and points of view.

5) Improvement of the Poverty Program machinery.

Reading told the churchmen that he did not believe that Oakland was "close to becoming another Watts," but that his program was designed to help forestall any such outbreak.

In support of his proposals, he said:

"I want to make the poor feel they are members of the community and have the feeling that they belong.

"I am only one man. I have to have the help of all of you, the Federal government, all the community, if we are going to achieve our goals.

"We must use this method, rather than the antagonistic method. We must work together."

In the Oakland context, this was something new. At first, the ghetto was skeptical—sure that nothing coming from City Hall could be trusted. Reading arrived at this position early because he was pushed by the threat of Alinsky and pulled by the EDA offer of assistance, but he also believed firmly in the program himself. As this became evident, the ghetto's skepticism was gradually replaced by hope.

97

Chapter VI

EDA in Action

At the end of February, worried about the growing antagonism between Negro leaders and the labor unions over the Skills Center and the Adult Minority Employment Project, I arranged a lunch with Bob Ash, executive secretary of the Central Labor Council, and Don McCullum, chairman of the Adult Minority Project. After Ash opened with an attack on the attitudes of the State Employment Service, I said, "Bob, I've got a real problem. My boss, Gene Foley, has committed EDA to a fifteen-million-dollar test project in Oakland. If I had to report to Washington now, I would have to say that we could not commit our fifteen million dollars with any prospect of success."

Bob Ash said, "But you don't have to report now, do you?" I replied that I could wait for a few weeks.

The most pressing problem was the Skills Center, which was vital to the success of the EDA program. Under the new Employment Plan procedure, each plan would specify the training needed for the new jobs. Sometimes this could be provided on the job. But for most of the hard-core unemployed, who would need a substantial amount of basic education in reading and arithmetic along with vocational training, a new

98

training school was required. The Skills Center recently established by the Federal government in Detroit provided a model for this.

But Detroit was very different from Oakland. The Detroit Skills Center had been designed to meet a shortage of workers in the automotive industry. It had the full support of the big automobile manufacturers and their one big union, the United Automobile Workers, which enabled it to overcome the basic weaknesses of the Federal training machinery. In Oakland, where there was no comparable employer support and much union opposition, these weaknesses were quickly revealed.

The Federal training statute, the Manpower Development and Training Act, divided the responsibility for each program among many agencies and failed to put any one in charge of getting the whole job done. Funds for training, equipment, and administration came from the U.S. Department of Health, Education, and Welfare, acting in California through the Vocational Education Division of the State Department of Education. Funds for subsistence payments to trainees came from the U.S. Department of Labor, acting through the California State Employment Service, which also selected the jobs for which training was to be provided, recruited the trainees, and placed them in jobs when training was completed. In areas of high unemployment like Oakland, EDA also controlled some funds for training and subsistence.

To operate a Skills Center, the State Department of Education contracted with a local vocational school or college. This institution was unlikely to be well equipped to deal with the five Federal and State agencies on which it was dependent both for its funds and for its policy decisions. Consequently, the plan to set up a Skills Center in Oakland had included an agreement that a strong local advisory committee would be needed to assist the contracting agency, in this case the Peralta College District.

After recommending in September, 1965, that a Skills Center be set up in Oakland, Anne Gould had worked closely with all the agencies involved in getting it started. One of her principal reasons for advocating that it be supported by a strong local committee was the attitude of the California State Employment Service.

Housed in an impressive, gleaming new office building flanking the State Capitol in Sacramento, its large staff had developed a strong professional pride in their procedures for job placement. These procedures had originated in the Depression, when many skilled union members were unemployed. They had then been adapted to the rapid expansion of California industry during World War II and the Korean War, when there was such a labor shortage that employers would take unskilled workers and train them on the job. The system was strongly oriented toward the attitudes of the powerful California labor unions and the apprentice training systems favored by them. It was not well adapted to cope with the present hard-core unemployed, especially against the opposition of some of the labor unions who had been its close allies for so long.

The Adult Minority Employment Project, initiated by Oakland employers and Minority leaders and staffed by the Employment Service, provided an excellent opportunity for innovation, but the Service could not free itself from its long established procedures. When I talked to its Director, Albert Tieburg, I found him sympathetic to the need for new approaches, but this attitude did not reach down to the staff. The first time I met Mark Johnson, regional director of the CSES in the Bay Area, he explained that the rate of placement in jobs was very low because the staff had been flooded with so many applicants that all its time had been taken interviewing them, and there had been little time left to devote to placement. When I suggested that it might be preferable to stop interviewing for a while and to concentrate on placing those already listed, he looked as if I had questioned some

100

fundamental truth, and replied simply: "That is not the way the Employment Service does it."

The Labor Department's announcement of a $4 million Skills Center in Oakland, to open April 1, had been released on February 15, despite Anne Gould's efforts to hold it up until the advisory committee had been named and an adequate list of jobs cleared for training. We agreed that EDA should do everything possible to remedy these defects.

On February 24, Andy Bennett, Blair Butterworth, Doug Costle, and I met with John Dunn, President of Peralta College, Walter Miller, who had just been appointed head of the Skills Center, and members of its staff, to learn all we could about their problems.

Miller, who had entered the vocational education field from the labor movement, was a hearty, bluff, strong-looking man, with a ruddy face and curly white hair. If the situation had permitted him to concentrate on the educational program, for which he was well qualified, I think he would have made a success of this job. As it was, the administrative complexities of starting a new program of this kind required different talents, if indeed they were not beyond solution by even the most experienced administrator.

John Dunn, tall, suave, and articulate, was the model of a college president. While he had heavy responsibilities elsewhere in a rapidly expanding community college program, he accepted the challenge of the Skills Center and gave it priority whenever the occasion demanded. Often, however, his energy and ability were not fully utilized, because Miller tended to put things in a good light until a crisis developed—then Dunn was called in to help retrieve the situation.

We met at the Marchant Building, just leased by the Skills Center. It was a modern industrial plant, built only ten years earlier and left vacant when a merger moved most of the company's operations to a different location. It had some serious drawbacks, not all of which were evident at first. It was lo-

101

cated at the intersection of three municipalities, Berkeley, Emeryville, and Oakland, with part of the large building in each. This meant that all alterations had to conform to three separate building codes and be approved by three sets of inspectors. Extensive alterations were needed, to provide partitions for classrooms in the large open floors and to add basement exits from the heavy equipment areas which could only be located there.

After a tour of the building, we spent two hours reviewing all the administrative problems. We emphasized the importance of the Skills Center to the EDA program and offered to be helpful in any way we could.

Dunn, Miller, and I then went on to a meeting arranged by Norvel Smith, at the request of several Minority leaders, to discuss the Skills Center.

At the beginning, there was intensive questioning about the Skills Center's present status and problems. Dunn emphasized that the only function of the Peralta District in operating the Skills Center was to provide training, according to established standards, for individuals recruited by the Employment Service and then turn them over to the Employment Service for placement.

When asked if the Center planned to use ghetto residents as teaching assistants, Miller said that the California State qualification requirements would exclude many ghetto residents who might, as a practical matter, be well qualified for these positions. Bert Corona said that there were many able to teach in the Spanish language who could not meet the state requirements. It did not occur to any of us simply to ask why the qualifications could not be changed for Skills Center positions. There is something about the way an established civil servant refers to "requirements" that dulls the lay listener into accepting them as infallible and unchangeable.

Norvel Smith brought up the need to appoint an advisory committee, to avoid having the labor-dominated Manpower

102

Advisory Committee continue to play the dominant role that it had in setting up the Center. McCullum pointed out that the Manpower Committee had had no Negro members until the previous December, and that the management members, selected by the Employment Service, were not strong and were outnumbered by Labor.

The idea of an advisory committee seemed new to both Dunn and Miller. Their first reaction was to suggest that the board of the Peralta District, as the contracting body, was all that was needed. This, I learned later, was a group of leading citizens, elected locally, who were well equipped to oversee Peralta's $40 million expansion program, but who were too fully occupied with that to become involved in ghetto problems.

Dunn finally agreed that a new advisory committee might be helpful. He felt that it should be appointed by the Peralta Board, but said they would welcome suggestions as to its membership. I said that, as the representative of EDA, a principal participant in the Skills Center, I wanted to be included in any discussions about the composition of this board. In my view, the board must provide a way of relating to and reaching out for the unemployed in the ghettos.

At this point Don McCullum suggested to Dunn that an appropriate group to appoint for this purpose would be the existing Adult Minority Employment Project Board and agreed to send him a list of its members.

As the meeting went on through dinner, we discussed the administrative complexities of the Skills Center and the difficulties of motivating the unemployed we must reach. Toward the end, Clinton White, who, using the methods familiar to him as trial lawyer, had been learning about the Skills Center for the first time by cross-examining Dunn and Miller, wrinkled his expressive dark face in puzzled despair, and said, "Pity the poor Negro. He's been rooked again."

In spite of all its difficulties, the Skills Center opened its doors to forty hundred trainees, all male heads of families selected by the Employment Service, in the middle of April. I visited some of the classes. Morale was high, and the teaching seemed good. One of the classes was taught by the Reverend James Stewart, a Negro minister I had met two months earlier. In the recess, he told me: "This is more exciting than preaching. I'm thinking of giving up my church to work full-time here." On evening visits to the Target Areas, we noticed that those attending the Skills Center wore their identification badges with pride when they went back home to the ghetto and held their heads high. One wished there could be more of them.

The only training available at the Skills Center when it opened was basic education in reading, writing, and arithmetic, and a few vocational courses—culinary workers, typing, and office equipment repair—carried over from previous programs. While the Central Labor Council had approved a substantial list of jobs in January—welding, auto mechanics, and electronic technicians, among others—each of these had to go through a long formal clearance procedure before funds were committed. Only then could equipment be purchased and teaching staff hired. It took the Skills Center staff about a month to write up a proposal, which then was submitted to a monthly meeting of the Manpower Advisory Committee. There, approval was often delayed to a later meeting while further information was sought. When cleared by the Manpower Committee, it went for final approval to two state agencies in Sacramento and to two, and sometimes three, Federal agencies in Washington. When a proposal got stuck on some desk along the way, it was often hard to trace.

Flatlands interviewed three Skills Center trainees:

Jonah Barron, cooking class: "I was born in Foreman, Ark. in 1931, in a small town by the name of Red River, on what they call the Hawking Brothers' farm. They owned all of these

104

plantations the Blacks rent. . . . We would bale hay and ride the cattle and feed them. . . . I started working with my father when I was seven. He was hated by everybody. He was a light Negro. . . . I was the oldest so I didn't go to school. We moved so often. The schools I went to, they were just church houses. Never did stay in one place too long. . . . I fought hard to get into the Skills Center. I was a gardener eight years for Richmond housing. The Unemployment asked me did I want to go into school. So they sent me into Contra Costa Jr. High for a twelve-week gardening course. But I couldn't make it— you had to know Latin names. I wasn't educated enough to understand. Most of the common names I know. . . . So then I got a friend of mine to write Unemployment for me. He made an appointment, and I went, and they signed me up for the Skills Center. . . . It did more for me than anything in the world. Brought me up in my spelling, reading, math, writing, and today they signed me up for a twelve-month course in cooking. I been going about eleven weeks now. There's people walking the street right now cause they's ashamed to say they can't read or write. But that's what it's for. To learn them. . . . As far as the Skills Center, gee, that's the most wonderful thing that ever happened for uneducated people. I never had somebody do that much for me before. . . . They got an unemployment office in the Center. They promised me if I stay and learn, they'll get me a job. . . . People got to eat as long as the world exists. When I learn it (cooking) I'll have a job for the rest of my life. If I don't make it, it's my fault."

Nathaniel Everett, electronics class: "I was from Alabama. Education, that's something I didn't get, maybe about the third grade. There wasn't any real schools there. I was in the same grade until I was fifteen, the third grade. . . . I left my home to better myself. . . . For seventeen years I worked with electricity in Mississippi, first digging holes for electric poles, then I went to wiring houses. My education, it didn't make no difference there. If you could do the job, you was the person for it. . . . I first came to California for a visit. It was pretty, and I went to work for a while. . . . I couldn't wire houses here. I think jobs here in Oakland—you have to have an education even getting a dishwasher job. Back in Detroit or New York all they wanted to know is could you do it. . . . You take the union here; you got to be in Local 304. The White person is working and the Negro is standing in the office—a wondering job. You don't find twenty persons belong to 304 without a job if they White. Mexicans and Negroes, you find thousands. . . . I had put in my application for here, and then there was an opening. I started must have been about June seventeenth. I been learning how to read and write and math. That's in the morning. The pre-volt electronics classes in the afternoons. It has did a lot for me so far. It brighten me up in my math which I didn't know nothing about. . . . When I finish I be able to go out there and probably get in the union—open a radio and TV shop. Got a year here for education and another year for occupational training. . . . I don't think you have to have a whole lot of money to start working on something. You can get a small business loan here. . . . Right now the Skills Center is filled to capacity because there is not all the rooms fixed. I got no criticism."

Fabian Trevino, machinist training: "I am from Mexico. I came to here two and a half years ago. I was in about four grades of school. We find some job but in the labor—not jobs that going to pay without a lot of heavy work. I was contracting in picking apples and things. The work was too hard, too dirty. When we get into the cannery we don't work hard, but we get more money. . . . After three months in a cannery I got laid off. So the Employment people they sent me to the Skills Center. We are eleven in the family. My mother is blind. Many people they want to come here—they go to the Employment Office, but I don't know why they been turned down. I learn

106

more English now, and arithmetic. Learning to read too. I want to run machines when I get out."

Those interviews show why the Skills Center, in spite of all its administrative problems, remained a vital source of hope in the ghetto. Since this hope could be realized only when ample vocational training was provided, this process led to some hard confrontations between the labor unions and the Minorities.

In the meetings of the Manpower Advisory Committee, the articulate and experienced labor members often seemed to be opposing the creation of new opportunities for Minorities. They frequently took the position that training should be limited to jobs where openings were available. The statistics on this subject furnished by the Employment Service were often incomplete and confusing. When delays lengthened, the Minority members became increasingly impatient.

For some jobs, where the labor contracts provided for apprentice training, the unions were reluctant to substitute accelerated Skills Center training, on the ground that poorly trained workers would have difficulty holding jobs. This attitude, while sincerely held, also seemed negative to Minority people, especially when it developed that automobile mechanics were required to take a four-year apprenticeship as compared to the two and one-half years required by the Civil Aeronautics Board for aircraft mechanics.

All of this, combined with the openly hostile attitude of the Building Trades unions, had put the Central Labor Council on the defensive. Their reactions reminded me in many ways of those of the businessmen and employers I worked with as a young lawyer in the thirties. These businessmen, confident of the rightness of their position and resentful at being blamed for the misdeeds of a few of their number, reacted defensively against criticism from the New Deal and from the militant labor movement. Too often, they tried just to protect their

107

position, instead of improving it by adapting to change and new conditions.

Early in February, Joe Chaudet, publisher of the *Labor Journal,* and Chairman of the Port of Oakland Commissioners, had asked me to address a weekly meeting of the Central Labor Council to explain the EDA program. We agreed on the date of February 28. As I thought about this talk, I felt rather tempted to add to my usual presentation a strong statement drawing a parallel between the idealism and human appeal of the labor movement in the thirties and the similar appeal of the civil rights movement today, and comparing the reaction of Labor today to that of many employers then. Hesitating because I didn't want to antagonize this group, whose support we needed, I was undecided when I went to New Lucky's Restaurant on February 28 to meet Bob Ash and the Labor Council staff for drinks and dinner before the 8 p.m. meeting.

I joined them at the bar, where we talked—of the Oakland general strike, and the West Coast labor movement. I soon learned that the Central Labor Council of Alameda County was a far more powerful body than the labor councils in the East with which I had been familiar. On the West Coast, strong local councils had developed at a time when the international headquarters of most of the unions were located in the East, four days away by train, and the local unions joined together to provide support not readily available from their distant international headquarters.

The full Council met every Monday night, and the Executive Committee met every Friday morning. No member union could strike without the sanction of the Council. Before strike sanction was given, a hearing was held by the Executive Committee at which both the union and the employer appeared. When a strike was sanctioned, the employer was faced with the pressure of the entire Council membership.

The staff of the Council negotiated contracts for over half

108

of the member unions. For the others, the larger ones which had their own negotiating staffs, the Council would move in with a top-level negotiating committee when requested, much as the international unions do in other parts of the country.

The Alameda County Central Labor Council reached the peak of its power in the late forties, just after the end of World War II. In 1946 it conducted one of the few general strikes ever achieved in this country. This brought everything in Oakland to a complete standstill until the union demands were met. The unity then achieved had later been fragmented, so that, in 1966, Labor was divided against itself, like almost every other group in Oakland.

The Central Labor Council included all of the AFL-CIO unions except the building trades. In most cases their record on Negro and other Minority membership was good.

The Building Trades Council, made up of the old AFL building crafts, was against opening job opportunities to Minorities in the high-paid skills, partly because there was a labor surplus in most of these trades, and partly one may guess, because they wanted to keep the openings in these high-paid jobs for their sons and nephews. However, in the lower-paid building crafts, the so-called "mud trades"—the Laborers and Cement Finishers—there were high percentages of Negroes and Mexican-Americans.

The two largest unions in the Bay Area, the Teamsters and the Longshoremen, having left the AFL-CIO, were also outside the Central Labor Council. Most of their locals had fairly high percentages of Minority groups, though here again, particularly in the case of the Teamsters, Whites held most of the higher-paid jobs.

Time and drinks passed quickly. Suddenly, it was 7:45 p.m., and Russ Crowell rose, saying, "Time for the meeting." Surprised and hungry, I said, "What about dinner?" The reply was: "Oh, we'll eat after the meeting."

Realizing that this was a form of hazing, I figured that if

they could run a meeting fueled with that many drinks and no food, I could speak at it. When we entered the Union Hall, filled with over one hundred local union presidents and business agents, Russ Crowell took his place on the high president's rostrum and called the meeting to order. He did me the kindness of calling on me first, ahead of the other speaker, a blind woman, an attractive blonde with a Seeing Eye dog, who was to make an emotional appeal for funds.

After describing the EDA program, still fired with courage from the bar, I went on to compare the position of the labor movement, as it had appealed to the college students of the thirties, when it stood for the dignity of man and for opportunity for the underdog, with that of the civil rights movement today, fighting for the same goals. I noted that in those days some employers had resisted change, and some had recognized labor as a new force with which they must negotiate for their mutual advantage. I said that it seemed to me that labor now faced the same choice in response to the demands of the civil rights movement. With labor's traditions, I said, I was sure they would not make the mistake many employers had made in the thirties, by fighting the Minorities' claims for dignity and opportunity, which were certain to win in the long run. Indeed, the labor movement could not afford to remain silent in this struggle, but must speak up and act to open opportunities to Minority groups. To my surprise, this was well received.

A week later, at the Port of Oakland, I saw Joe Chaudet, who had not been at the Council meeting. He clapped me on the shoulder with a big grin and said, "I hear you told us to get off our asses." I said I had tried to say it more politely than that, but was glad the message had come through. He replied: "It did, and it was needed."

In the meantime, I had been working closely with the EDA Washington team on the projects making up the complex Oakland EDA package, discussed at Dunsmuir House, of technical

110

assistance for planning, of public works grants and loans for port, airport, and industrial expansion, and of business loans. All other Federal programs in Oakland had been criticized for raising hopes and expectations in the ghetto, and then failing to produce results. EDA had said it would be different. To make good on this promise, we would have to clear all the Washington hurdles by the end of April—just two months away.

As I looked ahead, it seemed to me that the best way to get fast results for Oakland was to schedule another visit there from Foley, at a time when the projects were far enough along so that he would put pressure on his division heads for results which he could announce locally.

I knew such pressure was needed, because the Oakland program represented only a small part, less than 10 percent, of the total EDA budget, and project requests amounting to much more than the remaining 90 percent were coming in from all over the country. This placed heavy demands on the time of the EDA division heads. Their juniors on my Oakland team had no greater claim on their attention than dozens of others in other places. I was just a consultant, whose position carried no weight with them. While I was dealing with all of the Oakland projects as a package, with an internal set of priorities, they were comparing each separately with other projects all over the country. There was a real danger that they might downgrade some of the Oakland projects and approve those from other places instead, leaving the Oakland package full of holes.

Late in February, Foley had agreed to visit Oakland in the middle of March. There was no problem of persuading him, as he was eager to return to see how things were going. He began at once to put pressure on the Washington staff for progress on which he could report when he came. Much was accomplished, but the time was too short. The visit was put off until March 31, when the new Employment Plan procedure

111

would be ready for announcement, and some of the major projects ready for approval. Plans were laid for a joint press conference with Governor Brown.

Toward the end of March, however, the White House staff quietly placed a "freeze" on all large Federal grants, until a program could be developed to counteract the inflationary pressures of Viet Nam. We dropped the idea of a press conference, or any announcement, but Foley decided to come to Oakland anyway. We arranged a full schedule for him, beginning as soon as he arrived on the afternoon of March 31.

While I had already talked to almost everyone Foley saw, his visit was still an extraordinary experience for me and for all of us. In three days, he covered every segment of the community. He outlined the EDA program and the new Employment Plan procedure to each group, adapting the details of what he said to the interests of each audience. In the discussions, he was skillful in drawing out comments, and his excellent memory for names made a great impression. Their responses convinced him that in two months much progress had been made in bringing the different groups together to solve their common problems.

This visit, with the panorama of the Oakland scene it provided, and the sense of progress it created, was also a good morale builder for the EDA Oakland team, which had been working under such pressure. Of those who had been at the Dunsmuir House conference, Andy Bennett, Blair Butterworth, Doug Costle, Dick Daschbach, and Jay Schwamm were on hand. Floyd Hunter, whose research contract had just been approved, joined the party and came to all the meetings.

In these three days, Foley met about two hundred people in fifteen different groups and spoke to two hundred more at a meeting of the Council of Churches. The first meeting, on the afternoon of Thursday, March 31, made a deep impression on him. Presidents or business agents of the carpenters, plumbers, sheet metal workers, iron workers, and laborers

112

came to his room at the Boatel. They were young, personable, mostly Irish. Foley tuned in well with them, but in a long, searching conversation made no headway at all in enlisting their cooperation. They stressed the high percentage of Negroes employed in the Laborers, Cement Finishers, and other less skilled trades. Because of high-school and algebra entrance requirements, they did not hold out much hope for the higher-paid, more skilled trades, especially at a time when many of their members were out of work.

The next morning with three Negro leaders—Judge Wilson, Clinton White, and Don McCullum—Foley reviewed his discussion with the building trades. He tried out with them the possibility of a short-term program of local employment in the Target Areas on some street lighting and sewer projects, in place of trying to open up the construction jobs on the EDA projects. He ran into a stone wall. Clinton White's deep voice rumbled, "We can see no alternatives on this. We must break down all union barriers to Negro employment with every means at our disposal, and I mean every means. We will do this for the construction of all the EDA projects, even though we know that this may delay some long-term employment, and we will not accept any temporary made work as a substitute." The others nodded agreement. Don McCullum went on, "We have another problem with the unions. They think they have a stranglehold on clearing occupations for training at the Skills Center. We are going to break this, so that Negroes can be trained for all jobs where there are openings, no matter what the unions think about it."

The night before, Emmett Jones, the business agent of the Laborers' union, who represent the unskilled workers handling materials in building construction, had invited us to watch them sign in the next morning. We met him in the basement of the Labor Temple, the headquarters of the Central Labor Council, where several hundred men were being assigned to work at different construction sites. Nearly two-thirds of them

113

were Negroes. Afterward, we talked to Jones about the possibility of getting Negroes into the higher paid construction jobs, such as the Electricians and Plumbers, suggesting that a way might be found for Laborers to be promoted through on-the-job training. He held out little hope for this, since each union had its own apprentice training system, and there had never been any way of moving from one union to another in the building trades. After we left, Foley said, "You have to hand it to the Irish. When Paul Jones moved up to become president of the Building Trades Council, he still had enough political power to put his son Emmett in his place as business agent of the Laborers, and he's holding on to it as best he can. But this won't last long. Some day all those Negroes we saw signing in will wake up and organize to elect a Negro business agent, and then the Building Trades Council will begin to see things differently."

We then went up to the top floor of the Labor Temple to meet with the Executive Committee of the Central Labor Council, which had been holding its weekly hearing for employers and unions where strike authorizations had been requested. Foley outlined the EDA program of jobs and training, which aroused little interest. Dick Groulx, who was presiding, said that labor was interested in helping Minorities get jobs, "but it doesn't help a bit when rabble-rousers like Don McCullum go on TV and castigate labor for not cooperating." I suggested that labor's position was so strong that it need not be sensitive to criticism, and that the problem would never be solved until they could learn to work with leaders like McCullum.

We went on to a luncheon meeting at the Kaiser Center, to which Nils Eklund, vice president of Kaiser, had invited over forty top executives of leading companies in the Bay Area, including many from San Francisco. After Foley had described EDA's plans for Oakland, Eklund said that the Economic Development Foundation planned to raise a fund of

$1 million to provide its share of the local financing required under the EDA business loan program and would be approaching all the companies present for contributions. He then introduced Senator Knowland, who, we had heard, would offer to contribute $100,000 if nine others would do likewise. Knowland, after a strong statement about Oakland's needs, said that he would contribute $10,000, if nine others would do the same. Eklund leaned over with a stage whisper to say, "Bill, didn't you drop a zero?" Knowland rose and said, "That was a typographical error. I meant that I would do ten thousand dollars if ninety-nine others would do the same."

After lunch, we got in a bus with Mayor-elect Reading, City Manager Keithley, Port Chairman Joe Chaudet, and Ben Nutter and Monroe Sullivan of the Port staff, for a two-hour tour of all the public works projects of the port and the city, to give Foley a clear picture of what was involved.

Late in the afternoon, Foley, Doug Costle, and I called on Oakland's new Police Chief, Robert Preston, in his big office in the gleaming, modern new building of the Police Department. Taciturn and square jawed, he was very much a professional policeman. He had a good understanding of Oakland's problems, but a limited, conventional attitude toward solving them.

At 6 p.m., we gave a cocktail party—this Foley and I had to pay for ourselves, since the government doesn't provide for entertainment—for the Poverty Council members and other ghetto leaders like Curtis Baker and Elijah Turner. The Target Area members who had walked out of the Council two weeks earlier did not attend, but all the rest did. Foley's presentation of the Employment Plan idea was well received and the subject of many interested questions. Curtis Baker was in good form and to his, and our, surprise was complimented on his approach by Judge Wilson and Barney Hilburn, the Negro member of the school board, both of whom he had regarded as Uncle Toms.

We wound up the long day back at the Boatel, with Reverends Frykman, Moore, and Golder of the East and West Oakland Parishes, and Tom Fike, counsel for JOBART. Frykman was in one of his discouraged moods and had quite a chip on his shoulder. He began by sounding off against all Federal programs, and the way they were run. Looking around the room at the whole EDA group, he said, "The trouble is, you're all a bunch of phonies, trying to decide things behind your big desks back there in Washington. Maybe not Foley, or Bradford. At least they seem to try to find out what it's all about. But the rest of you don't, and are just phonies."

At this Andy Bennett rose, hair waving, and shouted, "And the same goes for you, Father."

Undaunted, Frykman went on to criticize the attitude of the Catholic Bishop of San Francisco toward Minority problems. Percy Williams, Foley's assistant, a Catholic and a Negro, responded with passion, emphasizing the need for effective Negro leadership, and the harm that could be done by antagonizing many who were ready to help the cause, like the Catholic Archbishop. He ended: "With friends like you, Frykman, the Negro needs no enemies."

The next morning, we met with the Fruitvale and West Oakland Target Area Committees. At each of these, Foley's explanation of the Employment Plan was received with interest and many questions. They accepted the idea that the Review Committee's role would be advisory, with EDA making the final decision, and were realistic about the statement that the hard-core unemployed might be able to qualify for only one-third of the new jobs created by EDA, that is, eight hundred out of twenty-five hundred, and that on individual projects they would vary from twenty percent to ninety percent, depending on the skills required by each employer. One woman said, "eight hundred is a lot more than none."

At each of these meetings and at the Poverty Council the night before, Foley said that he had met the Mayor-elect, John

Reading, and felt that he was a good man who wanted to solve Oakland's problems. Each time, this statement met a negative response. They doubted that any Mayor elected by the Oakland City Council could be good, or interested in solving Minority problems. Foley urged them to give Reading a chance to show what he could do, but their reaction was hostile and discouraging.

In the middle of the West Oakland meeting, in the dingy storefront office of the West Oakland Parish, a sports car driven by a White girl pulled up to let out Curtis Baker, who had come to sell Foley some tickets to a benefit for his recreation center. Muttering, "I promised him last night," Foley borrowed $20 from Andy Bennett and went out. One of the older Negro women inside grumbled: "What's he mean, wasting our time, going out and talking to trash like that."

Between the two Target Area meetings, we stopped at the Skills Center for a rapid tour of the new building and a review by Walter Miller of their program and problems. Because of the high rent on a short lease—they could not contract for more than two years—they had been urging EDA to buy the building, at a cost of over $3 million, to release their funds for training. As a business deal, this would have made sense, but the budgeting system works against using capital outlays to cut operating costs, and Foley decided against it.

Several things were accomplished by Foley's visit. The most immediately important, from my point of view, was that it firmly established the Employment Plan as the keystone of the EDA Oakland program. In approving it in Washington, Foley had acted against the advice of several of his division heads. When he exposed it publicly in each of his meetings in Oakland his own enthusiasm for it increased, and he became fully committed to it as a vital part of the EDA program, not only in Oakland, but throughout the country. The response of each group to the Employment Plan was favorable, in a way that lent credibility to the whole EDA Oakland effort. They ac-

117

cepted this as a new idea, created to meet Oakland's needs, which would lead to a practical, down-to-earth attempt by each employer to hire the hard-core unemployed.

Another good effect was to further a growing sense that Oakland's problems must be solved by local effort and by co-operation between local groups that had been antagonistic. Foley returned continually to this theme, and said that he could see real progress on this since his earlier visits. The fact that an Assistant Secretary of Commerce, with countrywide responsibilities, would spend three days in Oakland, talking to everyone, in itself encouraged this cooperation and created an atmosphere of readiness for the new Mayor's efforts in this direction.

Foley left convinced by his conversations in Oakland that the tentative program announced at Dunsmuir House two months earlier could succeed, with the addition of the new Employment Plan procedure. He was confident that the recent White House "freeze" on new EDA and other large Federal grants would soon be lifted. This was a Congressional election year, and if most of these grants were not committed in April and May, it would be too late to fund them out of the current year's appropriations. Before he left, we reviewed all the projects that were ready for approval, and agreed on the date of April 29 for him to return to make the announcement, jointly with Governor Brown and the new Mayor, John Reading.

The month of April was devoted to working out the final details of the projects with the Port and the city, pushing them through the EDA Washington mill for final approval, and preparing to announce them with appropriate fanfare in Oakland.

Work on these projects, which had moved rapidly ahead in the first part of March, had been slowed by the temporary freeze on grants—lifted during April—and by the preparations for Foley's visit. What had been accomplished in March

118

was preparation of the detailed applications and agreement within the EDA staff on the order of priority. All that remained to be done was to decide finally on the total funds available for Oakland, and to process the projects falling within this total through the remainder of the financial engineering, and legal review.

Foley took Doug Costle back to Washington with him to expedite this and called a meeting of all his division heads on Friday, April 8, to see what was needed to have all these projects ready for announcement on April 29. I remained in Oakland to keep things moving there.

My preoccupation with Oakland was soon jolted by a sharp reminder that what we were doing there had a direct effect on planning for the whole Bay Area. Dean Joseph Lohman of the Berkeley School of Criminology, who had been helpful in putting me in touch with the Berkeley faculty, asked me to come to Berkeley on the morning of April 7 to talk to Mrs. Clark Kerr, wife of the Chancellor, and to Martin Myerson, Dean of the School of Environmental Design.

Mrs. Kerr, an articulate and very positive lady, came right to the point. As an active conservationist and a member of a committee formed to prevent further land fill in San Francisco Bay, she wanted to protest the use of EDA funds to enable the Port of Oakland to fill in the large area to be occupied by the Seventh Street Terminal at the Oakland Mole. Having been active in conservation myself and long a director of the National Audubon Society, I was sympathetic to her general approach, and said so, but I could not agree with this particular application of it.

I pointed out that the Port's plan for filling this part of the Bay had been adopted before EDA was involved, and that work on it had been started under the regulations that existed then, before the legislative ban on all further fill. EDA's function in financing the new marine terminal there was to provide

119

employment for Oakland's unemployed, by the most direct means available.

Mrs. Kerr said that she regarded the Port of Oakland as a major threat and a very powerful force which operated without sufficient outside control. She felt that the Port should have been required to redevelop the dilapidated existing pier facilities along the Estuary instead of being permitted to create new land in the Bay. I replied that EDA had not had an opportunity to influence this choice, and agreed that in the future considerations like this should be part of Oakland's long range economic development planning.

I learned much later that another Federal agency had already financed a study, then being made, of the effect of fill on the currents needed to clear the Bay of pollution. This study supported the position taken by Mrs. Kerr, since the fill being put in by the Port carried the Oakland Mole out almost to the center of the Bay between Oakland and San Francisco. Better coordination would have brought that study to the attention of EDA in time so that we could have used the leverage of the large grants to the Port to shift the site of the marine terminal and avoid further fill in the Bay.

Back in Washington, final approval of each project required a mass of financial and engineering data from the Port and the city. Most of this had been filed with the original applications in February, but much additional detail had been requested.

Some of this seemed unnecessarily cumbersome, to me and to the Port and city officials. So it was, but this was unavoidable at this time. EDA was a new agency, operating with many procedures inherited from its predecessor, the Area Redevelopment Agency. The latter had been severely criticized in the past by the General Accounting Office and Congressional committees. Large sums were involved, and the need for speed in Oakland had to be balanced against the need to build records and new procedures which would convince future critics that the expenditures were being made prudently and in conformity with the statutory standards.

With hard work and long hours the processing of all the projects was completed by Friday, April 22. They were reviewed by the legal division over the weekend and were ready for Foley's signature on Tuesday, April 26.

Two last-minute hitches developed which nearly upset all our plans. The first was a long article in *The Wall Street Journal* on Monday, April 25. We knew that this had been in preparation for some time and had expected that it would come out after the announcement. It described the EDA Oakland program in detail, anticipating much of what the Governor and Foley planned to announce on Friday. Since the privilege of announcing grants of this magnitude, with the attendant publicity, is regarded as a political asset of some value, this article caused some momentary misgivings among the Governor's and Foley's staff. All finally agreed, however, that the announcement planned for Friday, consisting of hard news about actual grants, not just speculation, should receive ample coverage in local newspapers and on TV, and that no change in the plan should be made.

The second hitch was more serious. The form of the EDA grants and loans to the Port and the city was to be an offer, with conditions, which would then be accepted by the recipients. On Monday, April 25, Doug Costle dictated the final language incorporating the specific conditions which had been approved by the EDA lawyers over the weekend. When I took this up with officials of the Port and their counsel on Tuesday, it became apparent that they had serious reservations about the requirement that the Employment Plan provisions be included in lease and sales of Port property developed with EDA funds. Their counsel, who had not been a party to our previous discussions, seemed likely to recommend that the Port Commissioners reject these conditions. Some of the EDA staff in Washington, who were not happy with the Employment

121

Plan requirement, argued that agreement on this point should be reached with the Port and accepted by the Port Commissioners, before the announcement on Friday.

After this meeting, I called Foley to urge that we not try to obtain advance agreement from the Port, which might not be possible, but simply announce our employment conditions and leave it to them to accept or reject the entire offer. I was certain that once the offers had been publicly announced it would not be feasible for them to reject $23,000,000 of needed development funds because of the EDA requirement that jobs go to the local unemployed. Foley agreed. This worked out as expected. Both the Port and the city accepted the offers without question in the following week.

The press conference was held at 9 a.m. on Friday, April 29, in a large upstairs room at the Oakland airport. Foley, Governor Brown, and Mayor Reading met for coffee an hour earlier in a smaller room next door, to review the EDA program and to decide how to divide up the statements about it at the conference. They agreed that Brown would preside, introduce Foley, who would read the prepared statement announcing the program, and that Reading and Brown would then add their comments. At this point John Reading, who had been Mayor just three weeks, said to Foley and Brown that he was convinced that Oakland's greatest problem was unemployment, and that, while he welcomed the EDA program as one attempt to solve this, he was distressed because it did not go far enough. "It will provide long-term development, and permanent jobs in a year or two, but what is needed most is jobs now, this summer, jobs for young people, and for the unskilled.

"Unless more is done, quickly, we can have real trouble here in Oakland, anytime. It's bad now, and if Alinsky comes in, it will be worse. But there's nothing the city can do without outside help. Why can't the State or the Federal government

122

find funds for this, as was done in the depression of the thirties, with the CCC and the WPA?"

It was refreshing to hear this appeal from a Republican Mayor, but the cautious and negative response that came from the two Democratic politicians to whom it was made was depressing. They agreed that the need was great, but said it could not be met because of budgetary limitations and competing demands for funds.

When we had settled down in the larger room in front of the TV cameras, before an audience of reporters and officials of the Port and the city, the Governor introduced "Eugene Foley, the Assistant Secretary of Commerce for Economic Development, who has decided to conduct in Oakland a massive experiment in solving the principal urban problem, unemployment."

Foley then read his statement. After reviewing the background of Oakland's needs, he announced that EDA had agreed to offer public works grants and loans (40 percent of the total) amounting to $23,289,000, covering:

Airport hangar and support facilities	$10,650,000
Marine terminal and access roads	10,125,000
30-acre industrial park	2,100,000
Access roads to Coliseum area	414,000
	$23,289,000

He said that these projects would provide two thousand two hundred jobs when completed, and more later on, and that in addition $1,600,000 for business loans then being considered would create eight hundred new jobs. He outlined the new Employment Plan procedure designed to ensure that the maximum possible number of these jobs would be filled by the local unemployed, after training at the Skills Center, and referred to the contract with Floyd Hunter and his group for research, planning and evaluation in connection with all the projects.

As we listened, all of us who had been working on this felt a sense of tremendous relief. We had done all that we had set out to do, and more, and had done it on time.

Mayor Reading and Governor Brown each made brief statements welcoming the EDA effort to solve Oakland's problems. After some technical questions about the EDA projects, the reporters directed most of their attention to the Governor's decision, not yet announced, to run again. It was, for Oakland, a quiet meeting, because at the same time Curtis Baker and Mark Comfort were holding a press conference in West Oakland to announce the formation of the "Inter-city Committee to Bring Saul Alinsky to Alameda County," which drew all the ghetto activists. *Flatlands* quoted each of them:

Curtis Baker: "Saul Alinsky wants to be sure the Flatlanders want him. He doesn't care what the hill dwellers think.

"I have information of Saul Alinsky's attitudes and ways. I can't say his ways are like mine. I haven't seen the man in action. But if that man's name can make the Councilmen vote against his coming, I feel he might solve half my problems.

"Alinsky's going to start plenty of things tripping and running here. All that's dead in the Flats will come alive. This man's much more a worker for humanity than our President.

"We're tired of them damn suckers picking our leaders. It's just like that a White man never whipped a slave. He always got the Black man to do his dirty work for him.

"The people that's paying for Alinsky—they might hate us. But there's such a thing as respect. . . . I don't mind taking their money. The White man, he had my labor for nothing, so why can't I take his money?"

Mark Comfort: "There hasn't been no survey taken, so how can the so-called Black leaders say the people don't want Alinsky here? They afraid of the man for the simple reason they

124

know what the man can do. He's going to upset this here apple-cart. The man shakes them up. Scares them half to death."

That afternoon as Foley was leaving from the airport, we picked up a copy of the *Oakland Tribune*. Across the front page, the two big headlines were:

$23 MILLION GRANT FOR OAKLAND PUBLIC WORKS

Houlihan Indicted: $10,000 Bail

Foley shook his head and said, amazed, "I'll be damned. Just think, it's only three months, to the day, since he met with us as Mayor at Dunsmuir House. What a lot has happened since then!"

Chapter VII

Mayor Reading Takes Over

THE third issue of *Flatlands* carried an interview with the new Mayor, John C. Reading, on April 17. In it, he matched many of the other *Flatlands* contributors in frankness, saying:

I welcome the opportunity to sit down and talk with you. I realize of course no matter what I say I will be attacked merely because I am a member of the establishment.

On EDA: Nor is there enough minority participation in the labor trades involved in the capital construction projects. Still, any time you have a rush program you have to take what you can get.

On a human relations committee: I'd like to get this going within the next two or three weeks. I've got a meeting Wednesday, I hope, with Don McCullum, Clint White, and Carl Metoyer. I know these men are considered Uncle Toms by some. You have to start someplace. These men are educated. You try to pick the best person possible if you want to get the job done.

On the Poverty Council: Take the walkout for instance. They may have a point but this wasn't the way to get the job accomplished. They should have stayed within the committee and talked the thing over. . . . Using committees as a framework you come up with answers that represent the general good. We have to work toward the good of all rather than the wishes of the majority whether the majority be business, political, labor, or Negro.

On his open-door policy: Let's face it. There's a general reticence about coming into city hall especially among low-income groups. . . . I would be willing to go out to them rather than sitting here waiting for them to come to me.

On the City Council: I have a completely different philosophy than the former mayor. Every person has a right to speak in city council meetings whether or not they agree with me, provided they follow the established procedure. Every person will be treated with dignity, courtesy, and respect. In turn I expect them to treat the city council in the same way.

On Saul Alinsky: I don't like the idea. The avowed aims of his program are good. Organizing the minority and giving them a voice. The effects—the way it is worked out—you create a division within the city.

On himself: I am not a politician. I got into this by a fluke. . . . When the mayor's vacancy came up, someone had to accept the challenge. My chances of solving the problems were better than those of the other candidates. I had no alternative.

It's a thankless job. But every citizen has an obligation to contribute toward better government. When I as a business man try to solve a problem, I don't attack people to get a job accomplished. If you've got a business deal you sit down and work out a mutual meeting of the minds. I'm a business man, not a politician.

In the adjoining column an article by Curtis Lee Baker was headed, "HERE I STAND." It began:

I stand here today because I am suffering like my people that is poor, and you can do something about it.

We can talk and say all the goods in the world and do nothing about it. The world is lost, and men like me will make it a true hot hell to live in.

On another page of this issue of *Flatlands,* in a story about a "Protest and Defense Rally on Police Brutality in Oakland," Mark Comfort was quoted as saying:

We need unity to be strong, . . . all blacks and poor people. . . . We are beginning to learn we are somebody, and we are going to be somebody anyway we can . . . not Negro Americans, black Americans. . . . Brother, we've got to make it because we've come too damn far.

On April 7, John Reading had been formally installed as Mayor of Oakland in the high-ceilinged Council Chamber of the City Hall. It was a pleasant family affair, with introductions of his wife and children and those of Frank Ogawa, who became a member of the City Council at the same time. The occasion was marred only by the haggard presence of the outgoing Mayor, John Houlihan.

In the Oakland setup, the Mayor had the apparent responsibility of an elected official, but had no real authority except as a member of the City Council. The City Manager was the executive and administrative head of the city government, to whom all city departments reported.

The fact of direct election, however, and the need for leadership in solving Oakland's critical problems, made it inevitable that much was expected of the Mayor. This was reinforced by the nonpolitical nature of the City Manager's position, and by the approach of the new City Manager, Jerome Keithley. He preferred to keep out of the limelight and to concentrate on the difficult job of providing effective administration with severely limited financial resources.

While John Reading was willing to devote all his time to providing the leadership needed to find solutions to Oakland's problems, his capacity to do so was limited by lack of staff. The only personnel directly available to him were one admintrative assistant and three secretaries. He was fortunate in the administrative assistant, Jim Price, a young liberal with a strong social conscience and a warm sense of humor, who had attended theological seminary with Evan Golder of the West Oakland Parish. He had a real feeling for the needs of the

128

poverty areas, combined with a presence and personality which made it possible for him to deal effectively with businessmen and other government officials.

To supplement this small staff, the Mayor had to borrow help wherever he could find it. Not much could be expected from the overworked city departments, except on issues directly related to their primary responsibilities. His greatest resource within the city staff was John Williams, a Negro, the able director of the Urban Renewal agency. This agency had met many frustrations in dealing with the Federal urban renewal agencies, but the studies and projects it had prepared were the best available source of facts and ideas about Oakland. Williams's great ability and drive had created some difficulties for him with the older, more traditional city departments, but he worked well with Mayor Reading, and each helped the other.

Due to his position and ability, the other Negro department head, Norvel Smith, Director of the Department of Human Resources, should have been an equal help to the Mayor, but this never worked out. Smith was then so deeply involved with the problems of the Poverty Council and the Target Area rebellion that he did not have time for new ventures. Later the Mayor was moving rapidly into manpower development and placement activities outside the Department of Human Resources, where Smith felt they belonged, and some friction developed.

My assistant, Douglas Costle, formed close working ties with Jim Price, which reinforced my own good relationship with the Mayor. Both Price and Reading found that we could be counted on for impartial advice, based on a broad, though sometimes superficial, knowledge of the Oakland community, and for practical help in dealing with other Federal agencies.

Lastly, the Mayor could call on both the business community and on Minority groups for effective volunteer work on many projects. The same should have been true of labor leaders, but this did not develop.

129

The City Council caused some difficulties for the new Mayor, until he learned that many projects could be financed by Federal funding and operated by more representative committees, which he could appoint. But at the beginning, with a conservative majority unsympathetic to the Mayor's program, they were no help. On one occasion, in the middle of the pressure to bring Saul Alinsky to Oakland, they took the flatly negative position which Reading had wisely avoided, and adopted a resolution declaring that Alinsky was unwelcome in Oakland. This made them feel better, but it threw down a challenge to Saul Alinsky which nearly broke through his resistance to coming to Oakland at that time.

Alinsky retaliated by presenting a bundle of diapers "for the Mayor and the City Council" to a large Oakland delegation, headed by Curtis Baker and Mark Comfort. They had met him at the San Francisco airport where he was changing planes. Alinsky's message to the City Council, as quoted in *Flatlands,* was:

> So many of you are always asking, "Is Oakland going to blow?" But that isn't the issue. The issue is whether the people in Oakland are going to get the opportunity to join the family of American citizens. Are you going to sit home and worry about that or just sit home and wet these diapers worrying about Oakland blowing up?

Then, when Curtis Baker started to harangue the crowd, beginning, "I am Curtis Lee Baker, sometimes known as the Black Jesus," the gray-faced, blue-coated airline dispatchers at that gate thought they had real trouble on their hands. One of them came up and said, "Mr. Alinsky, your plane is ready," hustled him on board, and sent the plane out twenty minutes early, leaving many passengers behind. Alinsky later decided that Oakland had adequate indigenous leadership, and that the best way for him to assist them in getting concessions from the Mayor and the City Council was to remain outside—a threat of what would happen if they failed to act.

The Council's next contribution came when it heard that the Poverty Program investigating team—sent to Oakland by Sargent Shriver to look into the Target Area walkout—included a reporter from the *Los Angeles Times,* which had recently run a series of critical stories about Oakland. The Council passed a resolution declaring the temporary Federal official unwelcome in Oakland. This action was too much for Reading, who called the whole Council into his office, a most unusual procedure, told them privately what he thought of their resolution, and sent them back to the Council Room to repeal it.

The pressure for a Police Review Board was increased in the first part of 1966 by several incidents. The worst of these —one which might easily have triggered a riot—was reported in the April 23rd issue of *Flatlands:*

NIGHTMARE IN OAKLAND

Another Case of Police Brutality

EDITOR'S NOTE: the following are eye-witness accounts of what happened in the home of Luther Smith and his family, 1011 Campbell Street, West Oakland, early in the morning of Friday, April 8. The story these witnesses tell is one of police brutality. It is the story of how two Vice Control officers broke into the basement of the Smith house because they had seen two white boys leave and re-enter that basement and because the basement was in an all black neighborhood and next to a house where acts of prostitution (according to the police) have taken place. It is the story of how these Vice Control officers then collected some 25 uniformed Oakland police to "subdue" the three male members of the Smith household and bring them under arrest for defending themselves against the police. It is the story of how the Smiths, bewildered by what was happening to them, had nowhere or no one to turn to for help.

The Oakland police department charges Mr. Luther Smith Senior with having interfered with a police officer in the perform-

131

ance of his duty. It charges Luther Smith Jr. and Alonzo Smith with having committed battery against a police officer. It charges the two white boys with loitering under suspicious circumstances, refusing to give identification and resisting arrest.

The Oakland Police Department has refused to release to the defendants a copy of the crime report written up after the arrests were made. *Flatlands* was told that the Department is as yet unable to provide any information on the investigation it is conducting as a result of Mr. Smith's having filed a complaint of police brutality.

Flatlands therefore cannot offer its readers the Police Department's side of the case.

What happened to the Smiths might never have come to the attention of the community had it not been for the quick action taken by Mr. Curtis Baker after Mr. Smith, without lawyer, doctor, or funds for his sons' bail, called him for help. Now, however, the Smith case may well be the rallying point for a new and united drive by the people of the Flatlands to expose any prejudicial and brutal methods employed within the Oakland police force and to set up definite safeguards against their continued use.

LUTHER SMITH'S STORY
Mr. Luther Smith, Senior, resident of 1011 Campbell Street for the past 23 years:

I came home from work Thursday (April 7) about eight o'clock. I work at Todd's shipyard. So I was kinda tired. I didn't even take a bath. I got up there on the bed and laid down. Then about nine I got into bed, and I didn't wake up no more until it seemed like it were in a dream, and I hear my wife call me. I jumped out of the bed and started downstairs. "Wait a minute and get your pants," my wife told me. I slipped my pants on and didn't have no shoes. I could hear Lonny calling "Daddy, Daddy." Lonny and his two white friends had been in the basement. That's where we's got this neighborhood recreation center with a pool table, some weight lifts, and a record player. I ran out of the house and to the basement door. I seen one man punching my son.

Luther Junior—he was in the basement begging the men to get up cause Lonny weren't doin' nothin'. Luther had been upstairs

132

in bed. When he heard the hollering he went down the back stairs right into the basement. He beat me downstairs.

They had Lonny down on the concrete steps by the basement door. The door was wide open. One of them was laying right down on him and choking him. The other one was beating on his head. He didn't have no billy club. He was hitting him with his fist. I felt like picking up something and busting their brains out. But I didn't have no wind.

Lonny had just got his income tax return check. When I seed those two men I first thought somebody was trying to rob him. I had no idea this was the police.

I say, "What's the matter, what's going on?" He said, "We's police officers."

I say, "If you're police officers then get up off him. He'll stand arrest. He's not going anywhere."

Alonzo was pretty well out. I didn't see the two white boys no place. One of them had run upstairs and told my wife they's killing Lonny. I don't know exactly where the other white boy was.

I caught one of the men by the arm and pulled him up. He said, "I'm going to call for more help." Then he and the other one ran out there to the car. I didn't intend to start no fighting. I just wanted them to get up and talk.

Alonzo got up—there was a lot of blood on his face. I still didn't know whether they was police until them guys come in here with their uniforms.

I said, "Let's go upstairs." We came on upstairs. We had pitchforks up here. If we had to fight the police, we'd have something. But we had no intention of fighting.

The two white boys came back and knocked on the back door. "Nobody come in," I said. But Alonzo said, "Oh, that's my friends." So I reopened the door and they came in. When the police came in the front door I don't know what happened to them. I didn't see them no more.

It don't seem like it was more than a minute before we was upstairs when all them police got here. If it was the police that had come downstairs, I figured they were going to come in now and arrest the boys. I didn't figure they was going to come in hitting like that even after they kicked the door in.

133

As they came up to the door they says, "Let us in." My wife says what did they want. They don't answer nothin. They just knocked the door in and came swinging with billy clubs.

I was almost scared to death. I never seen nothin' like that. These guys after they got me, I figured it looked more like the Klu Klux Klan than anything else. If we had started any fight, they would have killed us all. About five of them jumped on Luther who was standing near his mother by the door. Some of them came at me, and some got Lonny when he was holding onto the chair.

They'll pick on our youngsters just for walking down the street.

They wasn't trying to handcuff us. They just trying to beat us. When I put my arm back like they told me, one of them just pulled both my arms back of my body straining my shoulder. He like to hurt me.

They beat us for a long time. My wife was begging them to get up off us. So was my daughter-in-law. We have another son, Glen. He ten years old. He seen it all. He didn't sleep a week.

After they handcuffed me they got me up. I said, "Would you let me get my shoes?" One of them said no.

Alonzo was still tusseling, holding onto the chair. I said, "Lonny, give up"—cause he didn't want to give up.

All that time they ain't explained nothin—just came in. I felt like they was going to beat us with the handcuffs on. They finally said that we's been fighting the police.

When we got to the station I asked for a doctor, and they said no. I asked for a phone call. They just acted like they don't hear you. I didn't make no phone call.

They put us in different cells. Lonny was just about out. He was in the cell next to me. We talked for a while. After a while he hushed talking. I called him and called him and didn't get no answer. Then I was scared. I figured he was dead.

I could hear the police. We was right there where they come in and out to the desk. "You go out this time and you bring in six. You don't come back until you bring in six." I hear them say to the ones that was going out. And they was going out to get them too. It weren't no joke. I seen the ones they brought back to the cells.

134

They kept us in the police station till 6 or 7 o'clock in the morning. Then they took us where we had to wait for x-ray, I mean thumb prints. I didn't get to make no call till 8. I called my wife, and the line was busy. I had to go in a room to wait for a call. The fan was up there blowing. It was cold. I shake the door until the officer finally came and let me out.

How I feel now is like that when I hear the sirens I wanta get my axe. They gonna have to kill me before they do it again.

I felt like these people was trying to start a riot. I understand they had the streets blocked off during the beating. The boys in the neighborhood—they tell me, "I wished I'd have been there." They's disturbed everybody in the neighborhood.

MRS. LUTHER SMITH:

This was what I first heard starting from the beginning.

There was a knocking on the basement door. I heard Lonny say, "Who are you?" I didn't hear the answer. Then he say, "Do you have a search warrant?" Again I didn't hear no answer. Then he say, "Well, get out." The next thing I hear was a big blunder and commotion down there and Lonny shouting "Daddy! Daddy!" He kept screaming like someone was killing him.

I said, "Luther, they're beating Lonny downstairs." He got out of the bed and started down with nothing on. I said, "Put your pants on."

I started downstairs too. I grabbed my robe. At that time you can't find nothin'. When I got to the bottom of the front steps I heard them in the house—my husband and two sons—so I turned and came back up the steps. I come in and fastened the front door. The white boy had come in between the time my husband went down, and I got ready to go down. I started down after the white boy told me they was killing Lonny.

My feeling was that someone had just broke in and was beating him up. You really don't know hardly what you feel. I felt like they might kill him.

When I came back up and fasten the door, I heard someone holler, "Open up or I'll kick the door in." These 25 policemen or so just walking up the front steps at me. One of them say to open the door and let us in. He was looking right at me. I say, "Well,

135

what do you want?" But he just start kicking. Luther Junior was standing beside me. My husband was standing in the background. They throwd both of them on the floor.

When Lonny saw them on his father he grabbed the pressure cooker. He don't know what he done. I know Luther Junior and my husband hadn't done nothin'. They was in the bed when the two men had come in downstairs.

My daughter-in-law, she's very nervous. When all those police in here beating on us she kept yelling, "What's going on? What are you doing to my husband?" One of them says to her, "Oh brawd, we've been watching this house for a long time."

My daughter-in-law called her brother. He took us to the station on 6th and Washington. They say they hadn't got no report about the arrests yet. We just waited there. They still hadn't booked them. The man at the desk told me, "You go start making preparation for bail." It was supposed to be an hour before they booked them.

In the police station I called the bailbonds man. Then I went to my husband's brother. There was still no booking report. Then we came home. Glen was still up. This was about 5 in the morning. After that I just sat there waiting for them to call. The first call was at 6 from Luther Junior. He told Van (his wife) to get him a lawyer. About 9:30 Luther Senior called. He say, "I'm sick as I can be." He say to bring his pills down here. He's a diabetic. Then I called to the police. I asked could I bring the pills in. The man told me, "We have medication here." Then I explained that Mr. Smith was a diabetic, and had to have pills every day. Anything can happen if he doesn't have those pills. I found out that man don't give my husband the pills until 9:30 Friday night when he got out of jail.

I got in touch with the bail man around 7:30 Friday night, when the booking was finally done. He told me Alonzo's bail was $16,500. Luther Junior's was $11,000 and Luther Senior's was $320.

Saturday morning my husband called Mr. Baker. He say, "I know Curtis. I knowd he was good." We felt like maybe Curtis could get the bail cut down. It wasn't long after he comes over here before the lawyers was here.

136

What I feel like now—if they get justice they won't be charged with anything. I don't know what will happen. Maybe the police department won't give justice. A police ain't supposed to just bust in your door without showing anything. If he come in dressed like your husband and don't show no badge or identification of nothing, how's you supposed to know who he is?

A police officer ain't supposed to try to kill anybody just because they's arresting them.

It's better for my sons to be here lifting weights in the basement than being out in the street. If a person can't do this at home without the police coming in, where can he go? After my eldest son got married, he say, "I'm going to teach my brothers to stay out of trouble—get them doing something." That's why he got all them things in the basement.

If the police carry on like they done, I don't want to live here no more. Where they can come in and beat up my family—I want to get out of Oakland. And I been living in Oakland for 24 years, and I has been a taxpayer for 22 years, and I never seen nothin' like this before. I was raised in Arkansas. I never saw any brutality like that there. Now I don't have no chance to tell nobody what's happened.

Robert Treuhaft, one of the lawyers who went to the aid of the Smiths, was interviewed by *Flatlands* on April 29. He said:

"We filed seven claims today, one for each of the members of the Smith family. The claims are preliminary to filing suit for damages against the city of Oakland, the Oakland police department, and the thirty police officers involved in the invasion of the Smiths' home the morning of April eighth.

"We had deliberately not filed a claim earlier than this. We are not planning to go through the police complaint route— where you file with the police a complaint against the police. We have no intention of asking the people who were guilty of this outrage to investigate the outrage. The case illustrates the need for an independent police review board, made up of civilians. We have no confidence in the police department."

137

Late in April, Mayor Reading asked the Council to resolve the Police Review Board question by setting up a Review Board which they felt would be satisfactory both to the police department and the Minorities. This would replace the independent Board voted earlier by the Poverty Council. The Council's response to this appeal was completely negative. Immediately after this Council meeting, Mayor Reading brought the Council members back to his office for a press conference, along with many community leaders who had been in the audience.

He opened the conference by warning everyone that Oakland could become "another Watts" unless the city acted promptly to improve communications with Minority groups and with the poor, saying, "the wall around City Hall must come down.

"The Poverty Council," he went on, "is ready to fall apart, unless the City Council acts to set up a Police Review Board." Many of its responsible members were ready to resign on this issue.

On the Alinsky question, the Mayor said he intended to propose to the Council of Churches that they spend part of the money that might go to Alinsky to hire their own organizer to work with Minority groups and the impoverished, who needed to have a bigger voice in city affairs. "It is not a question of City Hall being always right and they wrong," he said. "There are many things that we city officials have done to stir up tensions in this city."

He warned that the city must listen to these groups, and recognize that they had some cause for bitterness, saying, "I don't blame them. I'd be bitter too, if I'd been treated that way."

He concluded by saying that he planned to visit distressed neighborhoods to learn at first hand of their problems.

Shortly after this press conference, when I went to see John Reading to arrange for Foley's announcement of the EDA grants, I found him discouraged and doubtful as to whether it would be possible to solve Oakland's problems. This mood vanished as soon as he began to get results. In his first month in office, he had established a pattern which was to prove effective. As he identified each problem, his method was to propose a practical, direct solution, disregarding all difficulties and objections. He would then adapt this to meet objections, but persist until a solution was found.

His method definitely helped the Poverty Council to establish maximum feasible participation of the poor. At the March meeting of the Poverty Council, the "'maximum feasible" question had been referred to a committee headed by Don McCullum. Two months later, this committee worked out a recommendation which was discussed by the Council at its May meeting and adopted in June. This required that 75 percent of the membership of each Target Area committee should be "poverty persons" as defined in the law, and that this same percentage should be reflected in its delegation to the Poverty Council. The Target Area delegations would be a majority, twenty out of thirty-nine, of the members of the Council. To take care of the Mexican-Americans, a minority in each of the four Target Areas, a fifth Target Area was created, covering the same geographical area as the other four combined, whose proceedings would be conducted in the Spanish language. This ensured the Mexican-Americans of control, without violating the requirement that these committees must be open to all ethnic groups.

This was a significant victory for the Target Areas, though some of their representatives wanted to go further and give them direct control over project approval and staff appointments. One of the reasons it was acceptable to those originally opposed—the staff of the Human Resources Department and the middle-class Negroes—was that the 75 percent provision would limit the role of the White ministers of the East and West Oakland Parishes. Soon after this had been worked

139

out, Congress imposed restrictions on the discretion of all Poverty Councils in approving grants, and cut the funds available to them, depriving this ghetto victory of much of its meaning.

On the Police Review Board, Reading was less successful. At his suggestion in April the Poverty Council appointed a committee, headed by the City Manager, to recommend a solution.

In June *Flatlands* reported on a meeting of the California Civil Rights Commission, which met to discuss the problem:

Mr. Curtis Baker opened the hearings on police community relations with a call for a civilian police review board to meet the need for communication "between human beings and barbarians." As an example of injustice, Mr. Baker cited his own case of August 6, 1965:

A city councilman put Mr. Baker in jail for supposedly threatening him and calling him a "bald headed liar."

Mr. Baker told the Civil Rights Commission that "The police heads refuse to take a stand . . . to take responsibility into their own hands. Oakland must stop hiring Klu Klux Klansmen and Mississippi hillbillies to do their killing. We want some action in Oakland for the people who are in need and threatened."

Mr. Baker pointed out that when city officials do not have to give an account of their work something is wrong—"People not worried about their work don't have to worry about opening the book and turning the pages. We (Negroes in Oakland) are living in a cage."

In August, when no progress was being made, the Poverty Council revived the Police Affairs Committee which it had approved in February and requested that it be funded out of the Ford Foundation's grant to the City. The following exchange between two White businessmen on the Council, reported in *Flatlands,* shows why agreement was difficult:

Mr. Ennis: I object to all the time we spend on this ridiculous question of a Police Review Board. The more I read the more I am convinced what a fine Police Department we have here. I wish we could spend more time solving our parking problems.

Mr. Nicholson: The issue is not whether the Police Department is a good department. The issue is that a majority of the citizenry believe it is not receiving good treatment.

The City Council then directed the City Manager, as disbursing agent for the Ford funds, not to release money for this purpose, raising a serious question, since the Ford grant had designated the Poverty Council, not the City Council, as the body to approve requests for funds even though the city acted as custodian. The Poverty Council considered taking legal action to free the funds, but before this developed the City Manager's Committee, in January, 1967, completed a report recommending that a "Citizens Grievance Representative" be appointed, reporting to the City Manager, to receive complaints from citizens against all municipal departments, including the police, and investigate them. Mayor Reading promptly converted this idea into a proposal for an "Ombudsman" on the Scandinavian model and presented it to the City Council for approval. Without debate, the City Council voted it down, six to three.

In May and June, 1966, the Mayor began to visit the Target Areas, talk to the people, and attend many of their meetings. Both he and Jim Price maintained the announced "open-door" policy in City Hall. When Curtis Baker and many others tested this, they found that they were welcome and that they were listened to. All of this was done without fanfare or publicity, but the ghetto grapevine spreads news fast. We began to get reflections to the effect that the new Mayor "was not so bad, seemed to mean what he said," and was "trying to do a good job." Coming from those who had never before had anything good to say of the Mayor, they were significant compliments, and as time went on they became increasingly favorable. Early in July, Andy Bennett, Doug Costle, and I went to a meeting of the Fruitvale Target Area Committee to describe the Employment Plan procedure and ask them to designate a representative. We learned that Mayor Reading had met with the committee a week earlier and asked what kind of an impression he had made. All were eager to answer, and all the comments were approving:

"He came to see us, something no Mayor has done before, and was interested in what we said."
"He seems like a good man, who wants to do the right thing."
"He listened to what we had to say."
"He has problems too, and can't do everything."
"He is just one man, and has the City Council, which doesn't always agree with him."

From the time of our first meeting in early March, Reading had continually reaffirmed his conviction that much new employment could be created in Oakland by encouraging local businesses to expand, especially with the help of the Federal financing available from EDA and the Small Business Administration. The local structure created for this by Mayor Houlihan, the Oakland Economic Development Foundation and the Industrial Development Commission, had proved inadequate for this purpose. With characteristic directness, Mayor Reading took a new approach and then gradually adapted the old structure to it.

His first step, in June, was to organize a new committee of businessmen to arrange a series of seminars to acquaint local businesses with all Federal loan programs. Its chairman, Bob Mortenson, was an energetic promoter, who took the summer off from his own business to work on the project. By the end of June, his committee had proposed, and the Mayor had approved, an ambitious program for the months of August and September. This included three meetings of business executives, the first to be a luncheon meeting of about fifty from large companies, and the others to be seminars of two hundred to three hundred each from smaller companies. At each, the

142

available Federal support programs would be described, along with the Skills Center and other training. The final event was to be a "Job Fair" modeled on one recently held in Los Angeles, where a large number of employers would open recruiting booths to interview those seeking jobs.

At about this time, the City's Industrial Development Commission, set up two years earlier by Mayor Houlihan with an annual budget of $100,000, had come under fire in the City Council. It had done an apparently aggressive job of "selling Oakland" around the country, but had produced meager results. While some new business had come to Oakland during this period, more had left. The City Council was about to abolish it to save money. Instead, the Mayor persuaded them to continue it, with a shift in emphasis from seeking outside business to encouraging the expansion of local businesses and finding ways to retain those that were considering moving away.

Because he had built his own business in Oakland, Mayor Reading had a first-hand knowledge of the problems and knew how to enlist local interest and support. In working with the new committee, he held the planning meetings in his office, made the policy decisions himself, and paid close attention to all the details of how they were to be carried out.

Early in July, I attended the first of these planning meetings. Sitting around the Mayor's big office, representatives of EDA, SBA, and the Skills Center outlined their presentations. Agreement was reached on the format of the public sessions.

Former Senator William Knowland, publisher of the *Oakland Tribune* and new president of the Oakland Chamber of Commerce, was to chair each meeting and took an active part in this discussion. In the past, as a conservative Republican Senator, he had been opposed to large-scale Federal spending, but no trace of this appeared in his attitude toward Federal spending that would help business expand in Oakland.

143

When he had obtained a clear picture of what was available, he directed his attention to the two major uncertainties in the EDA business loan program: the danger of a narrow interpretation of the statute on the question of the availability of other financing, and the absence of a firm commitment on the amount available for loans in Oakland in the fiscal year 1966-67. He urged a "liberal interpretation," which was later adopted by EDA, and a maximum commitment, which was finally made in the amount of $10,000,000.

At the end of this meeting, Senator Knowland boomed out: "You'll have to have the wisdom of Solomon, Mr. Bradford, to solve Oakland's problems, but maybe it can be done." Pleased, I replied that I thought it could be done, but only through the combined efforts of all parts of the Oakland community.

The first meeting, a luncheon for sixty executives of large companies in the Kaiser building, was held on August 15. After outlining his program, Mayor Reading said his initial goal was to bring Minority unemployment down to the level of White unemployment, from over 10 percent to 4.5 percent, through business expansion in Oakland.

This was followed by two seminars, each attended by several hundred representatives of smaller firms. Before the first of these, the Mayor held a rehearsal for all the speakers at a box lunch session in his office. Don McCullum, who was to describe the Adult Minority Employment Project, said, "There is one thing we must get across to these employers. Many, many Negroes are now barred from jobs they are capable of doing, not by intentional discrimination, but by unrealistic job qualifications, which bar people with minor criminal records or those who lack high-school diplomas. If these requirements are relaxed, and qualifications are based on what is actually required to perform the job, many more Negroes and Mexicans can be hired through normal turnover, without waiting to create new jobs, or to provide new training." This approach, which could have an immediate, direct impact on Minority employment, appealed very much to Senator Knowland. In all of these meetings, he appealed to the employers to re-examine all their job requirements and revise them on a realistic basis. Coming from him, this advice had much more impact than it would have had coming from a government or Minority spokesman.

These meetings were effective in acquainting the local business community with the availability of government loans and the Employment Plan idea. With the Job Fair, they helped improve the climate for Minority employment in Oakland. Curtis Baker came to the second seminar, in beret and cape. When the talks were over, he rose with a question. Since the meeting was for employers, Senator Knowland, who was presiding, would have been justified in asking if he were an employer, and refusing to entertain his question if he were not. This almost certainly would have been done a year earlier. Instead, he listened and gave a fair answer, to two questions.

Flatlands concluded its report on the seminars by saying, "Much will depend on the personal understanding the Mayor is able to reach with businessmen. Personal contact—'holding a seminar over the phone'—will probably prove more effective in terms of changing employers' attitudes and thus their hiring requirements than any other aspects of the Job Program. This raises finally the most significant point about the program—that it represents the first positive effort on the part of the city and the Mayor personally to attack the worst disease afflicting Oakland's low-income and Minority citizens." This was followed by a full page of interviews, which included:

Ralph Watters, Kaiser personnel department: In the past, there was discrimination and all kinds of things. But today the major corporations are seeking to hire Minorities. The reason they're not employed today is that they're not trained. . . . We're guilty of discriminating in favor of Minority unemployed, but we don't want to have any charges made against us by Caucasians.

Evan Golder, West Oakland Parish: What's the key to the problem? Are employers willing to modify standards of hiring? One guy got up and said usherettes at the Coliseum have to have two years of college. The Mayor got them to change that policy. But it seems to me that the larger issue is that the Negro is in the place he is because we put him there. To get him out we're going to have to hurt a little. Business isn't willing to do this yet.

Gene Drew, Skills Center instructor and CORE chairman: What we said was that we wanted commitments from industry on jobs or there's no use. The city hall is contending they should have the opportunity to try this and we should trust them. . . . We're pointing out our apprehension to the Mayor that it's not going to result in Minorities getting employed. . . . The only way it can be done (besides a public guarantee of jobs) is through personal commitment. If the Mayor says it's being done that way we'll take his word.

Don McCullum: If the businessman wants to stay in business he'd better make certain changes to involve the Minorities in his work force. Minorities are consumers. . . . it's good business to have Minorities in your work force if you hope for support from the minorities for the product you're making.

Mayor Reading: I appeared before the Central Labor Council a week ago last Friday, and made a personal plea. They said they would take it under consideration and let me know. I never heard. I'm not optimistic. There's a lot more behind it than the fact that they weren't in on the initial planning.

I had lunch today with personnel officers of seven or eight of the major stores in Oakland, for a more detailed discussion of what would be expected of them in terms of the Job Fair and analyzing their hiring procedures. They agreed to have a representative of the Adult Minorities Project meet with them to examine their hiring forms and agreed as a group to review them and see what they could do not to lower standards but to make them more realistic.

In his column in the same issue of *Flatlands,* Curtis Baker was less optimistic: "Well, I don't believe most of these so-call leaders mean anyone that is poor any good. Black or

146

white. . . . The poor knows that they are suffering because the power's giving them nothing but hell."

At the end of August, on a trip to Sacramento, I called on Albert Tieberg, Director of the State Employment service, and told him of the Mayor's plans. His comment was: "Why should the Mayor be getting into this? Employment is not in his jurisdiction." I suggested that the unemployed were in the Mayor's jurisdiction, and that the Mayor's access to means of public exposure of the failures of those who had jurisdiction over the employment problem might spur them to provide solutions.

The Job Fair opened on September 24, a sunny Saturday morning, with a high-school band playing on the steps of the big Oakland Exposition Building, and speeches from the Mayor, Senator Knowland, Don McCullum, and others. Inside, one hundred twenty employers had set up booths, each manned with interviewers, stacked with folders, and decorated with posters and photographs about the company. It had been well advertised in newspaper, radio, and TV, and buses were provided on a half hour schedule from each Target Area. In two days, fifteen thousand came, thirty thousand interviews were held, and over nine thousand were scheduled for later interviews at company offices. Only 10 percent to 15 percent of these appeared for later interviews, which puzzled and disappointed the Mayor and his staff. *Flatlands* may have had the answer to this. In describing the crowd, it said, "Who came? Probably the most surprising thing was that very few people without jobs seemed to be there. Everyone looked well dressed and well fed; nothing like the weekday line at the Employment office a few blocks away." Many of those who had jobs may have been seeking better ones and found that the ones being offered were not enough better to follow further. The concrete results were that about three hundred were hired on the spot at the Fair and another three hundred after later interviews.

147

Disappointed at this small result, the Mayor moved promptly to set up a Manpower Commission to give continuing attention to all phases of training and placement.

Flatlands later ran an editorial on the Job Fair saying:

Business and industry must make room for the "qualifiable" as well as the qualified. They must also make room for those with "stripes"—that is, those with police records. Because a man has been arrested, even more than once, does not mean he has no goals.

One elderly man told me, "There is no need for me to go down there because I have a record. I have been trying so hard to make it, but they won't give me a chance."

"Most of them say you have to be over 18, and they want one or two years experience," Mr. Dominick explained. None of the firms he had talked to could tell him how to get the experience.

Mr. Bishop summed it up: "I want to find a job, that's all."

One of those who got a job on the morning of the first day at the Fair was Curtis Lee Baker, who had earlier been turned down for a position at the Skills Center, presumably because of his felony conviction, and the fact that he was out on parole. He arrived early in a business suit, without cape, cane, or beret and was hired as a personnel recruiter by the operator of a chain of filling stations, who put him to work on the spot in their booth. Seeing him there, Jim Price, the Mayor's assistant, stopped and asked for an interview. With a happy smile, Baker said, "No Whites can apply here."

Chapter VIII

EDA—The Program Applied

IN JANUARY, when I had agreed with Gene Foley "to help put the pieces together" for him in Oakland, neither of us knew exactly what this meant or how long it would take. After the April 29 announcement of the $23 million of approved projects, I left for the East thinking that my work in Oakland was about finished, and prepared to turn to other things. We had been so fully occupied in getting the projects approved in Washington that we had no time for thought about what would be needed to bring them to reality in Oakland. This began to take shape as I kept in touch from New York and Washington with Doug Costle and Andy Bennett in Oakland. In committing the funds, we had supplied the foundation. The local structure of training and jobs now had to be built, by the combined efforts of the city administration, Port officials, employers, labor unions, and Minority groups. This would not be done unless EDA continued to provide the initiative, as it had done during the first three months.

All of this would require a concentrated effort much like that of the first three months, but in circumstances where the dangers of indecision and delay would be greater, since the pressure of time provided by the budget deadline would be

149

absent. Soon after I returned to Oakland in the middle of May, I reviewed these needs with Foley. We agreed that I should stay on as a consultant for several months more, until these things were in shape to be handled through normal departmental channels.

Of all the difficulties, the most formidable was the need to overcome the resistance of the building trades unions. If their normal hiring practices were followed, very few of the higher paid jobs in the construction of the EDA projects would go to local Negroes or Mexican-Americans. The statutes and regulations requiring Federal contractors to provide equal employment opportunities for Minorities had never been enforced, except through the ritual of filling out "compliance" forms, in the Bay Area, or anywhere else. We knew that the EDA investment of $23 million was too small to provide any real leverage in persuading the unions to change their position, at a time when other Federal construction in the Bay Area amounted to nearly $1 billion.

For nearly a year, this issue had been dramatized in Oakland by the Committee for Justice on Bay Area Rapid Transit (JOBART) with demonstrations and picketing to demand construction jobs for Negroes. In April, Rapid Transit had started hiring without any commitment to JOBART, which accused it of building its system "with all white hands," after wasting a year in not training people in the area for these jobs, and threatened "direct action."

After he had failed to make any headway with the Oakland building trades unions in March and had appraised the local Negro reaction on this issue, Foley decided that we would have to take a firm stand on these construction jobs. Speaking to the National Council of Churches in April in St. Louis, where the Federal government was then making its first attempt to open the building trades to Minority employment, Foley referred to this problem in Oakland and said that he intended to take action there. A few days later, he repeated this to the top officials of the Port of Oakland in Washington.

Because the offers made by EDA on April 29 to the Port and the city contained a provision requiring advance approval by the government of the terms and conditions of each solicitation of bids for construction work, we all expected we would soon have trouble with the building trades unions. We didn't have to wait long. Early in May, the staff of the Central Labor Council drew up a proposal that three hundred Skills Center trainees be given pre-apprenticeship training and then preferential entry into the established apprentice programs of all unions. When they approached the building trades privately to persuade them to participate in this, Lamar Childers, head of the Building Trades Council, countered immediately with a public statement that his Council would not modify its contracts to allow for preferential hiring. He said, "Nobody objects to a graduate of the Skills Center or a high-school graduate or a Ph.D. for that matter applying for apprenticeship regardless of his color or where he comes from if he is qualified," and then warned his unions at a Council meeting against all attempts to force mandatory employment of pre-apprenticeship Skills Center graduates or of Minorities.

Since several months of architectural and engineering work would be needed before the Port and the city would be ready to solicit construction bids, Doug Costle and I decided to use this time to seek outside support. We learned that the Catholic Archdiocese of San Francisco had been studying the problem and reviewed their tentative program. The Bay Area Rapid Transit District approached us about Federal financing for some of their installations in Oakland, so we talked to them about it, finding that their principal difficulty grew out of a standstill agreement they had made with the building trades unions to protect them against strikes during their five-year construction period.

We decided that our best hope would be to bring together

151

all of the Federal agencies engaged in construction in the Bay Area, with current contracts of about $1 billion, the Rapid Transit District, with another $1 billion, and the major church groups, with many millions more and a strong moral position, to work out a joint strategy. We found that Aileen Hernandez, a member of the President's Equal Employment Opportunities Commission, who had come to Oakland in June for a hearing of the California Civil Rights Commission, was considering a similar approach. Bishop Pike, who was at the same hearing, said he thought the Episcopal and Catholic Churches would be interested in joining this effort.

Mrs. Hernandez then talked in Washington with Gene Foley and Ed Sylvester, Director of the Office of Federal Contracts Compliance in the Department of Labor. They agreed that the Labor Department should call a meeting in San Francisco.

The meeting was held on July 8, in a small conference room on the eighth floor of the austere Federal Building in San Francisco's ornate Civic Center. Gene Foley, as the senior Federal official, presided. With him at the head of the table were Ed Sylvester, for the Department of Labor, and Aileen Hernandez, for the Equal Employment Opportunities Commission.

The other Federal agencies represented were: the President's Committee on Manpower; the Justice Department; the Defense Department; the Department of Housing and Urban Development; the General Services Administration; the Twelfth Naval District; the Army Corps of Engineers; the Bureau of Public Roads; and the Civil Rights Commission.

The Bay Area Rapid Transit District sent its General Manager and two lawyers. The Archdiocese was ably represented by Richard Morris, the young lawyer who had developed their program, and Father Boyle, chairman of the Catholic Commission of Social Justice. Since the Catholics did not send a Bishop, Bishop Pike declined, but sent a representative.

Foley began the meeting with a statement of the problem.

152

Congressman Cohelan opened the discussion with a statement favoring equal opportunities and training for Minorities. Aileen Hernandez stressed the need for prompt action, especially in regard to the Rapid Transit construction. The Rapid Transit people reviewed the history of their situation, and reaffirmed their desire to find solutions, welcoming the support of as many others as possible.

Richard Morris described how the position of the Archdiocese had developed, in planning for the new Cathedral in San Francisco. Their approach was based on the moral premise that "no expenditures for church construction should be made for goods or services supplied by any person, firm, or trade union practicing discrimination in employment on the basis of race, color, creed, or national ancestry." After many discussions with other church groups and with contractors, they had prepared a draft clause to be included in all church construction contracts, requiring on-the-job training for members of Minority groups in the ratio of at least one trainee for each four Journeymen. This was still in the discussion stage and had not yet been agreed to by the contractors or the unions.

Don Roney of the President's Committee on Manpower warned that entry into apprentice programs would not solve the problem, since less than 10 percent of the journeymen in the building trades were graduates of apprentice programs. The balance came in as journeymen from outside the area, or were given cards by business agents on the basis of skill or friendship.

Ed Sylvester emphasized that the Labor Department's Contract Compliance Office had the responsibility of requiring fair employment practices as a major objective of each Federal construction contract. He said they would be prepared to consider a program of stiff advance clearance for each contract in the Bay Area.

In summing up, Foley stressed the advantages of coordinated

153

and planned action in this field. He suggested that all present report back to their principals and be prepared to come to another meeting in about a month to discuss a detailed program. In the meantime, he asked Don Roney to collect and distribute any available statistics on Minority employment in the building trades in the Bay Area and to work with Richard Morris in developing a program of action.

Throughout, the Colonel of Engineers, the Admiral of the Docks, and the Federal Highwaysman sat stone-faced and silent, not welcoming this intrusion of urgent, ill-defined, messy, social demands on the clean, engineering sweeps of steel and concrete which filled their visions.

After this meeting, Foley drove out to see some nearby Mexican-American towns in the Valley, where EDA projects were being considered. On the way, he stopped at Santa Rita Prison in Pleasanton to visit Mark Comfort, who was serving a six-month sentence imposed by an Oakland court a year earlier for his activity in a protest demonstration in December, 1964, at the plant of the *Oakland Tribune* over its Minority hiring practices. Out on bail, pending his appeal, during 1965 and early 1966, Comfort had done outstanding work with the Neighborhood Youth Corps of the Poverty Program and in a volunteer program with street gangs. A natural leader, he was one of the most forceful and effective of the young Negro militants in Oakland. He was ordered to prison in May, when the State Supreme Court denied his appeal, but obtained a stay to finish his campaign for the State Assembly in the Democratic primary.

On this, before the stay was granted, *Flatlands* reported:

Mark Comfort, candidate for the 15th Assembly district and well-known fighter for human rights, was called into court to begin a six-month jail sentence.

He was convicted by an Oakland court of "maintaining himself as a public nuisance and refusing to disperse at the scene of a riot" during a non-violent protest demonstration against the hiring practices of the Oakland Tribune.

Comfort appealed to the State Supreme Court who refused to review the case.

The court gave Comfort ten days to get his affairs in order before he goes to jail. Unless Comfort could win a delay, he was to go to jail Monday, May 16.

Mark Comfort says that he was a half a block from the sit-in when they arrested him. "They really wanted me badly."

"It's a pretty rotten trick to play on me," Comfort said. "I will not give in to this intimidation. The campaign is going real great right now. I'm going to continue right on through."

Asked if the jail sentence will hurt his campaign, Comfort replied, "If anyone tries to hurt you, it can help you."

Mrs. Comfort planned to carry on her husband's campaign in his absence. She says she will do everything she can to win.

When his campaign was over, on June 9, he was ordered by the Oakland court to begin to serve his sentence, though his appeal to the U.S. Supreme Court was pending. On June 22, because of this appeal, he was released by a stay ordered by Justice Douglas.

Foley, who had been interested in Comfort from the time of their first meeting in January, when Mark introduced him to the street gang he sponsored, the Almboy Dukes, visited him in Santa Rita to show his friendship and respect. A few weeks later, I was with Foley in Washington when he learned that the FBI had started a security investigation on him because of this visit. It was the only time I ever saw him really angry. A call to the Attorney General ended this foolishness, but the angry memory lingered on, and Foley spoke of it often with amazement.

The next meeting of the Federal agencies on the building trades was held in San Francisco on July 28, with most of the same participants, though the airline strike was making travel difficult, and some couldn't make it.

Representatives of JOBART, the militant group seeking job opportunities for Minorities with Bay Area Rapid Transit had asked to attend this meeting. We told them that it was a planning session, to which no union representatives had been invited, and that it would not be appropriate to include them. They had recently achieved a lot of publicity, on TV and in the newspapers, with a "watermelon eat-in" in a new railroad car that Rapid Transit had placed on exhibition, and apparently decided that our meeting could be used to bring them more.

When we arrived at the Federal Building there were about fifty JOBART pickets marching outside in the bright morning sun. They included Elijah Turner and Tom Fike among our friends from Oakland, and we stopped to chat with them before going inside.

At noon, after the end of our meeting, a delegation of these pickets, followed by a battery of TV cameras, came up to our floor to present to Foley a forty-five-pound watermelon as "soul food for delivery to President Johnson." Taped to its surface was a message urging the President to use his influence to make sure that Negroes and other Minorities got their fair share of jobs under the huge Rapid Transit construction program. It ended: "We hope that our message will become an organic part of you as you eat this watermelon."

At the meeting itself, Don Roney of the President's Committee on Manpower presented an analysis of Minority employment in the higher-paid building trades, confirming that it was very low. He then outlined a proposal for increasing Minority employment, to be tailored to the situation in each trade as to the skills required and the availability of work, and to provide opportunities for on-the-job training in specified ratios. This followed the basic pattern of the earlier program worked out by the Archdiocese, but had the advantage of adapting it to the conditions of the different trades. It provided that each contractors' association should draw up a

156

plan suited to its particular trade, to be approved by the government before contracts were awarded. This was in many ways similar to the EDA Employment Plan Review procedure and seemed workable, if the unions could be persuaded to accept it.

It was apparent to all of us that the next step should be a Cabinet level meeting in Washington to agree on a program which could be supported by a commitment from the White House that its implementation would be a prerequisite to all further Federal construction in the Bay Area, or elsewhere in the country. Armed with such a commitment, the appropriate agencies could sit down with the contractors and the unions to negotiate workable plans. Without it, no agency could afford to take a firm stand. It was agreed that the Labor Department should take the initiative in developing a detailed program, clear it with the other agencies, and call the next meeting in Washington.

It seemed obvious that no vigorous action in this field could be expected until after the Congressional elections in November, but we all felt that the program should be worked out in detail so prompt action could be taken then. The Labor Department went ahead, using the Rapid Transit application to the Department of Housing and Urban Development for additional construction funds—up to that time Rapid Transit had raised its own funds through bond issues—as the vehicle for preparing a program which would be a condition of granting the application. During August and September Foley kept in touch with Sylvester about this, and on October 5, called a small meeting in his office to consider the next step. I happened to be in Washington then. When I arrived for this meeting, Foley's secretary said he had been delayed at the White House, and that he wanted me to run the meeting. The others who came were Aileen Hernandez, Ed Sylvester, and Percy Williams.

Sylvester outlined the requirements which the Labor Department had drawn up for the Department of Housing and Urban Development to impose on Rapid Transit. They followed the plan outlined at our second meeting in San Francisco, and sounded satisfactory to us all. He agreed to circulate a draft to the group which had met there.

In closing, I stressed that no Federal department or agency could be expected to go out on a limb until the Secretary of Labor had obtained White House support for a program under which all Federal spending for construction in the Bay Area would be conditioned on the new employment procedures. Sylvester assured us that Secretary Wirtz was prepared to proceed along these lines.

After this, the guidelines which had been drawn up for the Rapid Transit District were incorporated in a "nine-point plan" which was sent to all Federal agencies engaged in construction in the Bay Area. This said the right things about Minority employment, but provided no new joint pressures for enforcement.

One of Oakland's many surprises was World Airways, the prospective tenant of the new hangar to be built by the Port of Oakland with EDA financing.

Its President, Ed Daly, whom Foley and I had met first in January, was a short, rugged man, who radiated power and drive, but whose warm Irish smile and quick eyes revealed an unusual sensitivity. When he left the Air Force at the end of World War II, he started a small nonscheduled airline, with some leased surplus planes, in Teterboro, N.J. In 1956, needing room to expand, he moved to Oakland, leasing a large, vacant hangar for a low rental. In his ten years there he had built up the largest nonscheduled, or "supplementary," airline in the world, with over seven hundred employees. He had based its success on providing quality passenger service, beating the major airlines at their own game in supplying charter planes and crews to large companies for "incentive" luxury trips for employee or dealer groups, to travel agency and other

158

"club" tours, and to the government for military and other personnel. In the preceding five years, his profits had risen from $500,000 to $7,000,000. He owned the entire company. Later in the year, he went "public," selling 19 percent of his stock for over $20 million, which meant that the whole company was worth over $100 million.

Confident that World Airways would continue to grow at an even more rapid rate, Daly predicted in January that his business would double in the next five years, and that he would need to add about eight hundred new employees, of whom over half would be aircraft mechanics, jobs for which he was sure the ghetto unemployed could be trained. There was a severe and growing shortage of mechanics in the industry, which could be met only by increased training. It should be possible to train the unskilled for these jobs, if they had mechanical aptitudes, in about a year.

As part of this expansion, Daly was placing orders for over $100 million of large new jets, including four of the giant four hundred to five hundred passenger 747s. To service these planes, he would need a much larger new hangar at the Oakland Airport. A large part of his business was providing servicing and repairs under contract for planes of other airlines. With a new hangar and the prospect of greatly increased traffic at the Oakland Airport, which was then operating much below capacity, this service and maintenance business would grow rapidly and provide employment for many more mechanics. Without a new hangar in Oakland, World Airways would have to move to an airport that could provide one. There were many cities all over the country ready to compete for this.

Daly wanted to stay in Oakland, though sentiment would not hold him there if he could not make a good business deal. He had grown up in poverty in a Chicago slum, understood its problems, and was deeply committed to helping others rise out of it. He had been the first to hire a Negro pilot, and his record on Minority employment was good.

By the time of the April 29 announcement, the framework of a three-way accommodation had been clearly established—EDA would make a grant and loan to the Port for building a $10 million hangar; Daly would lease the hangar for forty years for a rent which would cover the Port's financing and other costs, and increase with his earnings there; as part of the lease, Daly would agree with EDA on an Employment Plan to provide jobs for unemployed Oakland residents, who would be trained at government expense to qualify for these jobs.

I had shown the Employment Plan to Daly before it was adopted, and he had been enthusiastic about it. All that remained was to work out the details—the number of employees to be covered and the way in which they would be trained. The lease and the Employment Plan both had to be completed before EDA could make funds available to start work on the hangar, which it would take over two years to build.

All of this took over six months of intensive work, from May to October. There was never any doubt of the outcome, since everyone involved had so much to gain. The only question was how long it would take to put all the pieces together.

While we were struggling to reconcile the views of four Federal agencies, EDA, the Labor Department, the Department of Health, Education, and Welfare, and the Civil Aeronautics Board, which licensed aircraft mechanics and prescribed the training requirements for them, I was surprised when a fifth appeared on the scene, in the form of three officials of the Bureau of Indian Affairs, who came to a meeting in September to tell World Airways about their program for bringing Indians from reservations to the Bay Area and training them for jobs. They said proudly that they had already placed ten thousand—I thought grimly that this was about the number of unemployed Negroes in Oakland—and that they had four hundred more in training at that time. They offered to

160

set up a program to train fifty to one hundred aircraft mechanics for World Airways—mostly Indians from Alaska, "where they see more of airplanes than they do in the Southwest"—who could be trained in local vocational schools for longer periods than the two-year maximum at the Skills Center and in other similar programs. They suggested that these young Indians might make better aircraft mechanics than Negroes from the Oakland ghetto.

At this point I broke in to say, "This has been very interesting to me, and I have learned a lot I didn't know about the Bureau of Indian Affairs program. We have a problem here, since we must reconcile the conflicting aims of two quite different Federal programs. Your statute was designed to bring unemployed Indians from their reservations to cities and other places where there may be job openings, and train them for these jobs. The EDA program was designed to bring jobs to the places where the unemployed reside, and train them there. To do this, EDA has financed some industry near Indian reservations. I would agree with you that for each unemployed individual, the important thing is to get a job, not the way the government helps him get it. But I cannot agree that your Indians should have preference in getting jobs with World Airways.

"In Oakland," I went on, "the EDA investments are being made to provide jobs for unemployed residents of Oakland. World Airways is preparing an Employment Plan committing it to this purpose, to justify EDA's investment in a $10 million hangar which it needs. EDA could no more tolerate the importation of Indians from reservations to take jobs at World Airways than it could tolerate the importation of union members from outside Oakland to fill these jobs. If World Airways wanted to do this, we would not build their hangar."

The Bureau of Indian Affairs people agreed that under the EDA program, Oakland residents must have priority. They suggested that, if a sufficient number of trainees could not be

161

found in Oakland, World Airways then consider coming to them to provide jobs for Indians.

By October, it was agreed that World Airways would set up and operate the training program, with the government paying the cost, apart from the Skills Center, partly because it would be better to locate it at the airport, but more because the Skills Center was still suffering from administrative confusion. Anne Gould brought all the Washington agencies together to work out with the Civil Aeronautics Board a new set of training requirements, which shortened the training period from thirty to nine months. This was done by separating the airframe and power plant specialties into two different courses and jobs, and by eliminating requirements for training on nonmetallic frames—learning how to glue fabric to wood —and propeller power plants, which was not needed by mechanics who would be working exclusively on jets. The nine-month course would not produce licensed mechanics, but would qualify the trainee to start work at World Airways, and he could then obtain his license after a period of training done part-time outside of working hours.

This program was then incorporated in the Employment Plan, which was approved in early November. By then, World Airways' projected personnel needs for the five years 1967-1971 had risen to 1,764, double the original estimate, of whom 1,295 would be aircraft mechanics. While the new hangar being financed by EDA would not be completed until 1969 or 1970, World Airways agreed in the Employment Plan to begin immediately to give preference to qualified residents of Oakland in filling new positions. It was expected that the new training program would start early in 1967 and would begin to qualify trainees for these positions before the end of the year.*

* As this book was about to be printed, I was astonished to learn that the proposals for this training program, the brightest hope in the EDA experiment, had remained entangled in the bureaucratic jungles of Sacramento and Washington throughout 1967, and were still hung up there in June, 1968.

In May, when we began to move ahead with the Port projects, we found that the staff of the Port, and especially its head, Ben Nutter, continued to have serious reservations about the Employment Plan procedure, which had not been negotiated with them, but imposed as a condition of the EDA offer. Their reaction was similar to that of some of the EDA Washington staff, a feeling that this was a strange new device which might make it difficult to lease or sell the property developed with EDA funds. While they realized that this property could not be developed without EDA, and that the purpose of the EDA grants was to create employment, they feared that the Employment Plan might cause prospective tenants to seek sites in places other than Oakland, where there were no such restrictions. In practice, we found that most tenants, once they understood the Employment Plan, welcomed it as a clear-cut, affirmative solution to the problem of Minority employment, with which they were inevitably concerned, in response to state and Federal fair employment laws, and as citizens of communities with large and growing Minority populations.

In this effort, two additions to the EDA team in Oakland were very helpful. Iverson Mitchell, from the business loan division, came out to replace Dick Daschbach, who had resigned to go into business as a consultant. Mitchell was an experienced negotiator, who had worked on EDA projects all over the country, and who was confident that much could be done to bring in large companies looking for new plant locations, in addition to helping local businesses to expand. The other was Fred Scott, who was in charge of equal opportunity enforcement on all EDA projects in the western area served by the EDA regional office in Seattle. He came to work in Oakland on all the first Employment Plan negotiations, which would set a precedent for much of his work elsewhere. In working for many years with the California Fair Employment Commission, and later on a special task force assigned to relieve tensions in Watts after the riot there, he had developed

163

a mature understanding of both ghetto and employer attitudes.

Both these men were Negroes. When I made some of the first introductory visits with them, I realized that there was a marked advantage in having these negotiations, whose purpose was to increase Minority employment, conducted by Negroes. In their presence, most employers came to grips much more quickly with the realities of training and employing unskilled Negroes. They seldom looked for token solutions, as many had done when talking to me alone. This reinforced one of the main advantages of the Employment Plan procedure— the positive approach which a businessman naturally took when asked to show what he could do to justify the government decision to make a favorable loan or lease to him.

We delayed setting up the Employment Plan Review Board until the dispute between the Target Area Committees and the Poverty Council was settled in June, since this might have upset our method of selecting the Board.

In the meantime, we went ahead negotiating Employment Plans with World Airways and with a number of the companies to which EDA was making business loans. Since this was a new field in which there were no precedents, these plans required much time and thought. Several of the employers objected to the penalty clause which made noncompliance with the Employment Plan a default enabling EDA to terminate a lease or call a loan. In a forty-year lease or a fifteen-year loan, this seemed to place the employer at the mercy of unknown future administrators who might act in an arbitrary or unfair way. After thinking about this, I began to explore the idea of arbitration, with which I had been familiar in labor contracts, as a means of settling disputes over compliance.

Doug Costle worked with the legal staff of the Labor Department to draw up arbitration language which might be included in the EDA leases and loan agreements. As I studied this, and looked into the California law on arbitration, it became clear that arbitration was preferable to the harsh penalties of default. The arbitrator, if he found that an employer was not complying with the Plan, would issue an order directing him to comply. If the employer refused, a court order could be obtained directing him to comply, with stiff financial penalties if he did not.

At about this time, I attended a meeting of the Fruitvale Target Area Committee, to explain the Employment Plan procedure to them and to ask them to nominate a member of the Review Committee. Since we had not yet agreed on the arbitration provision, I described the default machinery. In the discussion which followed, one of the Negro women active on this committee said, "Let me get this straight. You have some employer, who files a Plan saying he will employ twenty of our people. We approve his plan, and he starts up with your money. But then he chisels a little bit, and only employs eighteen, and takes two others from outside, maybe his cousins or something. Does this committee then say, 'You fire those two, and take on two of ours.' And if he won't, then you call his loan, and put him out of business, and the other eighteen lose their jobs? I don't like the sound of that." In a few minutes, she had cut right to the heart of the problem we had been struggling with for months. I told her we were worried about this too and that we were working on something better, so a court could order him to carry out his plan and fine him if he did not, without putting him out of business. We finally decided, at the end of August, to substitute arbitration for the default clause.

The Employment Plan Review Board was to have eight members, one from each of the five Target Areas, and one each from labor, management, and EDA. Ken Thompson, who had been at Dunsmuir House and had been close to all that EDA had done since, agreed to serve as the management member. The Central Labor Council agreed to designate Norman Amundsen, a tall thin Norwegian with a scholarly manner, who had been a member of the staff of the Coun-

165

cil, but had left it to teach at Berkeley. The Spanish speaking "Fifth Target Area" appointed Cesar Flores Mendez, a sturdy Mexican-American businessman. The members from each of the other Target Areas—Mrs. Ruby Baker, West Oakland; Mrs. Jewel Manley, North Oakland; Mrs. Willie Thompson, Fruitvale; and Mrs. Marjorie Woods, East Oakland—were all Negro housewives. This was not surprising, since the majority of the Target Area Committee members were Negro women, who played the most active part in their meetings. Fred Scott was much concerned about this and felt strongly that the Review Board should include at least two Negro men, one of them young, to give it a better balance of viewpoints. Don McCullum made the same point in a different way. He said, "Brad, the Mexicans, labor, business, and EDA are all represented by able men, experienced in negotiating, who will be able to snow the four women." I agreed that a better balance would be preferable, but felt that we should not interfere with the Target Areas' right to select their own representatives. Scott and McCullum undertook to work with the Target Area Chairmen to see if some substitutions could be made, but the first meetings of the committee were held before this had been done.

In fact, these four women proved to be excellent committee members. They did their homework, studied the Plans in advance, and asked searching, practical questions. One of them, Mrs. Thompson, visited the plants of several of the employers incognito, talked to employees, and formed her own impressions.

The impact of this committee on the employers who presented their plans at its meetings was interesting to watch. They all came with constructive, positive ideas about what they could do to help provide jobs for the hard-core unemployed. Some of them went far beyond what any outsider would have suggested, such as using the parole board and state prisons as a source of referrals. As they responded to the questions of the committee, a desire to do more was aroused. Preconceptions were put aside, and replaced by a problem-solving response. The Target Area members helped this along by being realistic about the capacities of their ghetto neighbors and their needs for motivation and training. I realized, as I watched this, that we had opened up a new way of harnessing the capacity of businesses, both large and small, to solve this problem in a way that government enforcement procedures could never do.

The first meeting, to organize the committee, was held on the evening of September 8, in the big ground-floor show-room off Jack London Square which was the EDA office. Gene Foley was able to come and emphasized the real innovation in Federal employment programs represented by this new Employment Plan Review Board procedure, which would set a precedent for use nationally.

The next meeting was held on October 8, to review three Employment Plans. The first was for Bennie's Candies, a small family business that made peanut patties, headed by Bennie Smith, an elderly Negro. With an EDA loan of $55,000, he hoped to expand, to meet the growing demand for his product and to add thirty-three new employees in three years. When asked if all his employees would be Negroes, he replied with dignity that the jobs would be open to all who needed them. The next Plan approved was for Rainbow Car Wash, to borrow $135,000 to add thirty-five employees at a new location. Its owner, Angelo Sposeto, said to the committee, "Let's face it. I pay low wages. You have to in this business. But I take boys who have dropped out of school, or who come out of prison, and train them. It doesn't take a lot of skill, but they do have to learn how to do it and, especially, how to work as part of a team. After a year's experience with me, they go on to better jobs, that they couldn't get without this experience, and I expect this. I'm sort of a training school where they learn how to work and hold a job." The last Plan considered was

167

Colombo Bakeries, an old Oakland firm run by an Italian family, which manufactured sour dough "French" bread. Expanding in a new plant with a loan of $423,000, it would add fifty workers, to be trained on the job.

At its third meeting on November 12, the Board approved two Plans. The first was based on a loan of $241,000 to Sierra Cotton Mills, which reported that thirty-five of its forty-five hourly employees were from Minority groups. It planned to add sixty-six over two years, and to provide on-the-job training. Its president, Gilbert Roberts, said, "For many years, I have worked closely with the parole officers at San Quentin Prison in hiring those who come out of prison. They are the really hard-core unemployed, believe me. Our experience with them has been good. They are glad to have a steady job, and want to show they can make good at it. After they have established a good work record with us, many of them move on to higher-paid jobs somewhere else."

World Airways sent a large delegation to the meeting, headed by its executive vice president, Brian Cook. They reviewed recent developments and current expansion plans, which indicated that over one thousand aircraft mechanics would be added in the next five years. A number of questions were raised. Mrs. Thompson said she had tried to visit the hangar, but had been turned away by security guards. Cook invited the whole committee to make a tour. Amundsen and Mendez asked about the effect of security requirements on employment, especially with respect to arrest and conviction records. World said that on some jobs they had to be guided by government security requirements, but that they went behind records on an individual basis and had a number of employees who were on parole. The training program was not yet in final form, but would be added to the Plan as soon as it was ready. Amundsen said that in this case the Board had to place some faith in the employer's good intentions, so that

168

work could go ahead on the hangar, and that it would be able to check on what was being done at later meetings.

My last appearance as a consultant for EDA was to act as chairman at the November meeting of the Review Board. Approval of the World Airways Plan, by a Board that had learned to function well, rounded out all that I had set out to do when I began in Oakland in January, nine months earlier. It was time to go. While I picked up my papers and looked around the familiar office for the last time, I thought of Gene Foley, and of our parting in Washington the month before. On October 5, I had spent the day in Washington, talking to Foley and others about what remained to be done in Oakland, making a full report to the Secretary of Commerce, John Connor, and having a long interview with a reporter for *The Wall Street Journal*. At the end of the day, I took on the meeting on the Building Trades in Foley's office. He had to miss this, his secretary said, because he was "stuck in a meeting in the White House," but wanted to see me when he came back. After the others had left, I stayed on in the newly furnished office, watching the brilliant autumn sunset beyond the Washington Monument.

Foley came in, rather breathless, and sat down. He said, "What I'm going to tell you has to be kept in complete confidence, until it becomes public, which it will soon enough. The President has just accepted my resignation, which he will announce tomorrow."

I knew that he had submitted his resignation in August, because he felt that he had been in government long enough, and wanted more time to be with his family, and a chance to earn a better income for them.

"I had said," he went on, "when I put in my resignation, that I would be willing to stay on until after the election in November, if that was what the President wanted. He has accepted it now so that Ross Davis, the EDA Administrator, can be nominated as my successor and approved by Congress

169

before adjournment. I will stay on with the government until the end of the year as a White House consultant on ghetto problems. Before that, I will travel with the official party on the President's trip to the Pacific, and I am leaving tomorrow afternoon on Air Force One for Manila as part of the advance group to make arrangements for his visit there in three weeks." We sat and talked quietly for a while, as he readjusted to this sudden decision, and agreed to get together during the morning to talk to Ross Davis about Oakland.

Walking back to my hotel through the twilight, past the White House, I thought, "It takes men like Gene Foley to get things done in government, and there aren't enough of them. It's a shame to lose him now, but good that we have carried the Oakland thing as far as we have. Not much will be added to it now, but maybe enough has been done so that it will work and set a pattern for others like it."

The next morning in Foley's office it was a hectic scene, as he told his top assistants about the change. I joined him in a conference with Buckminster Fuller, who had an appointment to talk about the future of the cities and had appeared before he could be reached to cancel it. We talked for nearly two hours. Foley was frequently interrupted by urgent phone calls and visitors. After each interruption, Fuller would resume in mid-sentence and carry on. He talked of the city of the future —of a design he was doing for the Japanese for a city in one building, two miles high and two miles across, housing a million people, and floating on water—of a Dymaxion dome which could enclose Harlem, housing its residents in the supporting structures while the rest was rebuilt. In spite of his preoccupations, Foley entered into this discussion with enthusiasm, telling Fuller of his hopes for building an enclosed city in Minnesota, or in Alaska, and of what the Russians were planning along these lines in the Arctic.

We then spent an hour with Ross Davis, talking mostly about Oakland, as Davis in his two months as Administrator

170

of EDA had already become familiar with all of the other EDA operations except Oakland, which Foley had handled directly himself. After lunch, I said goodbye to Foley, and he left for Manila.

The next day, Friday, I had a long talk alone with Ross Davis. He was a tall, quiet, reserved man, with none of Foley's enthusiasm, but with a well organized approach based on broad experience in government. He agreed that much was at stake in Oakland and asked me to draw up an outline of what remained to be done. I told him that I thought my work there would be finished in about a month, and that Doug Costle could carry on for only a few months after that, since he wanted to join a San Francisco law firm. He arranged for me to meet Charles Patterson, then one of the top officials of the Peace Corps in Washington, who had come to see him about the possibility of working in Oakland. Patterson, after working for the Peace Corps in Africa, had decided that, as a Negro, he would like to shift his attention and efforts to the problems of the Negro at home, in the ghetto of an American city. He had grown up in the Bay Area and had a Ph.D. in sociology from Berkeley. When I talked to Patterson, I thought he would be an excellent choice to represent EDA in Oakland, which he later agreed to do.

Then I talked to Anne Gould and Andy Bennett, who were still shattered by the shock of Foley's sudden departure. I assured them that Oakland would still have a high priority and that our program there would continue to go forward. It might be less exciting from now on, but it would probably be better organized.

Chapter IX

The Mayor and the Federal Government

In August, 1966, Senator Abraham Ribicoff of Connecticut, chairman of the Senate Subcommittee on Executive Reorganization, held a number of hearings, at which the Mayors of many cities testified on the problems faced by their cities in their dealings with the Federal government. Several of these Mayors were sharply criticized by members of the committee for their limited grasp of the problems in which they were involved. Oakland's Mayor, John Reading, appeared before the committee on August 24, 1966. His testimony was well received. In it he said:

The directions given me by Senator Ribicoff's secretary were to speak directly to the subject of how local government can gain maximum effectiveness by coordinating existing Federal, state, and local funds to accomplish specific goals.

Oakland is a typical core city with the core city's typical problems—problems which to a large extent can be traced to the well-known exodus of large numbers of white middle-class citizens to the suburbs.

Federal assistance programs forge a major weapon to attack

these problems. At present, Oakland has one hundred forty different programs and projects which have some form of Federal funding in their budgets. Total current Federal expenditures for development, education, and rehabilitation total $87,424,052. And in the next five years, the total Federal investment is expected to amount to $378 million.

These are all good, in fact excellent, programs. However, their maximum effectiveness can only be achieved through coordination. . . .

He then outlined the many steps that had been taken locally in this direction, with varying degrees of success. He criticized the red tape and delays involved in Federal grant programs and advocated substituting a system of direct grants to cities, without any strings attached, to permit more orderly local planning.

In conclusion, he said:

May I say that I do believe that we are making progress, although I recognize that our present programs have many weaknesses.

But I am concerned, too, about the future effects of the influx of new minorities into our northern cities and how fast we are moving at the city level to cope with these incoming tides.

We cannot wall our cities. We can only increase our efforts to improve them. This will take better-planned and better-coordinated programs.

In his five months in office, Mayor Reading had earned the right to speak with feeling about "the real need for some mechanism to tie together . . . the multitude of Federal, state, and local programs," and for "better-planned and better-coordinated programs." He had decided to concentrate on finding ways to meet Oakland's greatest need—jobs for the unemployed. He was able to move swiftly to organize locally the businessmen's seminars and the Job Fair. But when he turned to the Federal and state agencies on which he must depend for recruiting, training and placing Oakland's jobless, he found much conflict and confusion:

—EDA, which had shown that it could process $23 million of public works projects in six weeks, couldn't tell him whether a business loan of $100,000 could be approved in six weeks or six months, and it had not been able to decide how much it would allocate for business loans in Oakland or what some of the important eligibility requirements meant.

—Two state and three Federal agencies had become embroiled in such a bitter dispute over funds and training requirements for the Skills Center that many felt it would have to close down.

—The Adult Minority Employment Project had been crippled by the dispute between the Employment Service and the Central Labor Council, which was proposing that a new agency be created to replace it.

—The Poverty Council had settled its internal problem of 51 percent representation for the Target Areas, but the future of many of its needed projects for training and education in the ghetto was in jeopardy as Congress attacked the budget and administration of the Poverty Program.

When Mayor Reading returned from the Ribicoff committee hearings, it was evident that his experience there, and the favorable comparisons made by the committee and by the press between his approach and that of the Mayors of many larger cities, had increased his determination to find new solutions in Oakland. While he did not say so, his actions from then on indicated that he intended to run for reelection when his term expired in April, 1967. His earlier moods of discouragement and hesitation disappeared, and he began to take command.

The East Bay Skills Center, which opened its doors to four hundred trainees in the same week that Mayor Reading took office, had been in a state of recurrent crisis ever since. Long delays in clearing jobs for training meant that almost all of these trainees had to be continued in basic education for many months more than they needed, while they waited for their vocational courses to start. At a cost of $500 per month per trainee this, together with the high cost of building altera-tions, two years' rental, and equipment—all of which, under the peculiar government accounting regulations, had to be written off in the first year—raised the total cost per trainee well above the $4,000 guideline established in midsummer when appropriations were being cut.

The problem came to a head in August, when current funds for the Skills Center were delayed while the Federal and state agencies controlling them met in Sacramento to resolve the issue. On August 25, the day after Mayor Reading testified in Washington, the Skills Center's director, Walter Miller, made a dramatic appearance at a well-attended Manpower Advisory Committee meeting to announce that the Skills Center would run out of funds at midnight that night and to ask the committee to appeal to the Governor for help. Seeing that some of the Center's trainees and staff were present, he added, rather lamely, "You should not view this with unnec-essary alarm." A few calls to officials in Sacramento released the funds, without involving the Governor. Restrictions were imposed on the average amount that could be spent on train-ing, which Peralta College felt might limit its ability to reach those who needed training most, who lacked basic education, but John Dunn called a press conference to reassure everyone that Peralta would not abandon the Skills Center and would adjust as best it could to the new rules.

August was a month of increasing tension in the Oakland ghetto. *Flatlands* reported a number of serious police incidents, one of which came close to starting a riot. For seven weeks Luther Smith, whose home had been invaded by the police on the night of April 7, had been picketing City Hall with signs urging a Police Review Board. *Flatlands* covered this lone crusade, and others joined him. Under the heading: *"7th*

175

week—Luther Smith Marches On" he was quoted: "I believe there's really gonna be a riot here in Oakland. . . . I heard over the radio that the police department was ready for anything, shotguns, blockades—I dreamed that a bunch of youngsters had started a riot and they had set Oakland on fire. I dreamed that I was worried to death about I wanted them to get out of it, big guns going off, and I didn't want that. I have had lots of youngsters, White and Colored, come by and talk to me while I have been demonstrating. They told me that I was demonstrating out there for nothing. They didn't think that would break it at all. I asked them to come and help me. They said, 'No. The only thing that's gonna break it would be a riot.' And I tole them, we don't want that."

One of the basic flaws in the Skills Center concept was that it had no responsibility for placing those it had trained, but merely turned them over when training was completed to the Adult Minority Employment Project and the State Employment Service, which at that time were not in a position to be effective. Knowing that failure to place its graduates in jobs would discredit the whole operation, Anne Gould persuaded the Skills Center to employ as a placement specialist Hugh Taylor, whom she had met when he was doing successful work in this field for the California Fair Employment Commission. He was a valuable addition. A Negro who had grown up in poverty and worked his way through college and law school, he had a deep understanding of the problems of ghetto residents. The Employment Service resented his appointment as an encroachment on their jurisdiction. When he persuaded several large employers—who had stopped using the Employment Service because of their bad experience with it in the past—to take Skills Center trainees after a few weeks of prevocational training and enter them in company training programs at no expense to the government, the Employment Service opposed releasing them on the ground that this would "skim the cream from the vocational training programs." Anne

176

Gould's comment was: "Cream kept too long can get pretty sour," but the Employment Service insisted that Taylor be kept from interfering with their responsibilities. In an article headed, by coincidence, "Cream of the Unemployed," *Flatlands* added: "Unless adequate funds are forthcoming in the very near future, the Skills Center might become a monument to bureaucratic bungling—a skeleton staff of instructors with a lot of Federal and State officials running around wondering why all the trainees left the Skills Center."

Members of the Skills Center staff were quoted in *Flatlands:*

The Department of Labor appears to be deliberately making it tougher for institutional training to do its job. The projects that we have written and submitted for approval seem to become bogged down in administrative red tape and all this after we were besieged by all kinds of Federal and state top brass to get the Center going. We have it going, and it is going fine, but UNLESS WE GET SOME OCCUPATIONAL TRAINING PROJECTS APPROVED IN SHORT ORDER, THE PATIENCE OF THE MINORITY IN OAKLAND WILL WANE.

As if it did not have enough other troubles, the Skills Center in September became briefly, but intensively, involved in the campaign for the governorship of California. The Republican candidate, Ronald Reagan, suggested to Mayor Reading that he would like to appear at the Job Fair when it opened on September 24. Fearing that the candidate's presence would distract the participants in the Fair, the Mayor suggested that instead he visit the Skills Center, for which the Mayor wanted to enlist his future support. Hearing of this, the Central Labor Council, which was supporting the Democratic candidate, Governor Brown, picketed the Skills Center, in great force, on the day of Reagan's visit. The scene which followed, well covered on local TV, didn't help anyone. The candidate had to force his way through massed pickets to enter the Center. Many of the pickets followed him inside, disrupting the classrooms which he visited with cries of "We want Brown." Dick Groulx of the Labor Council, who had never been a strong supporter of the Skills Center, gave a tough interview on TV saying that labor resented having the candidate "use our Skills Center for political purposes." Reagan, as he went through the pickets to get in and out of the school, could think of little to say, but at least he kept his temper, which several of his aides did not. He sent Hugh Taylor, who had been his guide, a note saying, "I very much appreciate your kind hospitality last Friday for what was certainly a memorable afternoon. I'm very sorry to have brought such confusion and chaos into such a fine school."

Busy with other things, I had not realized how much all these difficulties were impairing the Skills Center's development. In October, I arranged for a visit to Oakland by the personnel directors of some large electronic firms meeting in San Francisco, so that they could learn about its available facilities—the industrial park being financed by EDA; the business loan program for employers locating there; and the Skills Center to train the large pool of unemployed local residents. We hoped they would be persuaded to recommend that their companies locate new plants in Oakland.

After they had seen the industrial park and the Skills Center, I talked to two of this group, vice presidents of large, expanding companies in the aviation field. I told them about the EDA business loan program and the Employment Plan requirement, which they found acceptable, and then asked what they thought of the Skills Center. They said frankly that they did not receive a favorable impression. It appeared to be badly administered and badly laid out. They estimated that nearly $1 million must have been spent in remodeling and putting up partitions, but these were badly designed and were not soundproof, so that instruction in one room could be heard in the next.

They regarded the industrial park and the EDA business

loan program as extremely favorable factors in relation to plant location. So was the existence of a large pool of unemployed labor. But the quality of the training witnessed at the Skills Center was so poor that this negative factor would outweigh the favorable factors in recommending a decision to their companies.

In reporting this to Ross Davis, I said, "The reaction of these two knowledgeable executives is very disturbing, and confirms Anne Gould's reaction after her last visit, on which she based her recommendation that the aircraft mechanic training be located outside of the Skills Center. It underlines the need for a concerted effort by Mayor Reading to get this on the right track and to appoint a high-level Advisory Committee which can follow it closely."

During October, when the results of the Job Fair had been compiled and studied, the Mayor was disappointed at the small number actually placed in jobs—about six hundred out of the fifteen thousand who attended. By then, he had learned a great deal about the operations of the State Employment Service, the Adult Minority Employment Project, and the East Bay Skills Center. When Anne Gould and I went to talk to him about these results, he said, "I am just amazed and appalled at the confusion of agencies involved in this employment thing, and the total lack of any central direction."

Building on his experience with the businessmen's seminars, he decided to make a strong attempt to provide order and direction in the manpower field. He and his assistant, Jim Price, drew up a proposal for a broadly representative Manpower Commission, to "develop a comprehensive program in the field of recruitment, training and placement of the unemployed and underemployed persons in the City of Oakland," and to coordinate the activities of all organizations involved in this. Realizing that its success would depend on strong staff direction, they asked if EDA would be able to finance a new position of Manpower Director in the City Manager's office

179

for this purpose. We agreed promptly, since we had already earmarked funds for strengthening job placement activities, and were pleased when Hugh Taylor was later selected for this position.

The Commission proposal was presented to the City Council in November and approved in January. The Mayor immediately appointed a representative Commission of eighteen members, with Carl Metoyer as chairman. Hugh Taylor became its executive secretary. Two months later six members of this Commission were appointed to be the core of a thirteen-member Advisory Committee to the Skills Center. Another subcommittee of the Commission was named to work with the State Employment Service and the Adult Minority Project. At last the problems of these agencies seemed to be on the way to effective solution, through a powerful local initiative which might be able to overcome the inertia of Sacramento and Washington.

In working with the city administration on these problems, Doug Costle and I realized that it could not succeed in bringing the Federal agencies together unless some new mechanism for this purpose was created by the Federal government, locally and in Washington. We had begun to lay a foundation for this soon after the announcement of EDA's $23 million investment in Oakland. In Washington in May, I went to see Robert Wood, the Under Secretary of the new Department of Housing and Urban Development. I urged that his Department use the EDA pilot program in Oakland as an excuse to move promptly on its projects there. This new Department had just been formed by combining more than a dozen existing agencies, and at that time its administrative problems were immense. Legislation designed to enable it to experiment in new concepts of urban development, the Demonstration Cities Bill (its name was later changed to "Model Cities" when "demonstration" became an increasingly ugly urban word), was having severe trouble in Congress. The Department was under such pressure to do things in so many cities that it was difficult for it to act experimentally in one city, as EDA had done in Oakland.

I suggested to Wood that the EDA pilot project in Oakland might justify a special effort by his department there, to achieve maximum impact for several Federal programs in one city. He was interested in this idea and called a staff meeting two days later to consider it. At this meeting, Doug Costle said that what was now at stake in Oakland was "the credibility of all Federal programs in the ghetto." Wood asked his staff to consider the possibility of using the Bay Area Federal Executive Board as an "umbrella" for joint Federal action and agreed to assign a special representative to work full-time in Oakland.

I then talked to Roger Wilkins, Director of the Community Relations Service in the Department of Justice, which had the responsibility of working with police and ghetto leaders to reduce tensions. He listened with interest to the Oakland story and said he would consider assigning a representative there.

On the same Washington visit, I called on Sargent Shriver, Director of the Office of Economic Opportunity, which operated the Poverty Program. I told him about Oakland and how closely we had worked with the Poverty Program people there. I also reported on our talks with Wood and outlined our ideas for bringing all Federal agencies in Oakland into an effective working relationship.

During the summer, Alan Cuthbertson was appointed "Metropolitan Desk Man" in Oakland by the Department of Housing and Urban Development, and Ed O'Connell was assigned to work there by the Community Relations Service. They both moved into the EDA office. Cuthbertson, a former city manager, began to develop with John Williams, director of the city's Urban Renewal Department, a set of priorities for all of Oakland's housing and urban renewal projects, most of which had been pending for several years. They had been held up in part because of "Proposition 14," passed by the voters of California two years earlier, which repealed the State's fair housing law, and caused a freeze to be put on all Federal housing projects in the state. The state Supreme Court had just held that Proposition 14 was unconstitutional, so it was possible to move again. Also, the Model Cities legislation, which had been moving slowly through Congress since January, seemed likely to pass in the fall, and Oakland hoped to be one of the first cities to qualify under it for a sizable demonstration grant.

Ed O'Connell, who had worked behind the scenes in Watts and several other cities during and after the recent riots, established contacts with the Police Department and with a broad range of ghetto leaders, seeking ways of relieving tensions and forming ties that would be useful if trouble came.

We told these two about all that we had learned in Oakland, went with them to Target Area meetings and formed a friendly working team that needed no directives from Washington to promote cooperation.

Following up on our talks with Wood, Doug Costle became the EDA representative on the Federal Executive Board for the San Francisco Bay Area. These Boards exist in most large regions of the country, and are made up of the principal representatives of all Federal agencies in the region. They have no formal coordinating authority, but are encouraged by the Chairman of the Civil Service Commission, who is responsible for organizing them, to meet regularly to exchange information, establish good personal relations, and discuss common problems. They frequently set up subcommittees to consider subjects requiring joint action by several agencies.

Costle persuaded the Board to have its "Critical Urban Problems Steering Committee" prepare proposals for joint action by all agencies involved in urban problems—EDA; Housing and Urban Development; Labor; Health, Education and Welfare; Office of Economic Opportunity; Small Business

Administration; President's Committee on Manpower; and Community Relations Service. In September, this Steering Committee approved a proposal, prepared by Costle, to set up a Task Force, composed of representatives of all agencies concerned with Oakland's problems, to draw up an overall plan for the most effective use of Federal money in Oakland and the establishment of an effective Federal-city relationship. Once this plan was approved, each participating agency would allocate to the Task Force the funds required, and it would make the decisions on individual projects, subject to veto by the agency concerned. The report began:

The crisis faced by the Federal Government in the cities is a crisis of credibility; neither the Congress nor the poor see any results. The Congress does not see any overall improvement either in statistics or the riots. The ghetto resident has found that neighborhood organization does not feed his family and that jobs created by Federal money for the long-term unemployed will be unavailable for a year or two, and that regular job openings are unavailable to him for lack of training or union discrimination.

The Federal Government must face the total problem of the city and its residents and must administer its programs as if it were facing one problem with many aspects and many remedies, not many problems which happen to concern the same place and the same people. The object of the Federal Government should be to change the ghetto and the life of the people in it, not simply to create jobs, encourage better schools and renew neighborhoods. One program alone will not change the future of the average ghetto resident.

To attack the total problem of the cities and to demonstrate the effectiveness of Federal programs, a concentrated effort must be made by all Federal agencies concerned with cities in a limited geographical area where the Federal funds available could produce concrete results.

The Federal Executive Board endorsed the Task Force proposal and asked the participating agencies to obtain approval from their departments in Washington for the assignment of personnel on a regular basis, and for contributions to a modest budget for a research and planning staff. EDA and the Department of Housing and Urban Development gave their approval in November, and by March all of the others had agreed. When Charles Patterson was appointed by Ross Davis in November as his special assistant for the Oakland project, one part of his assignment was to head the staff of the Task Force.

John Macy, Chairman of the Civil Service Commission, attended a meeting of the Federal Executive Board in San Francisco at the end of September and undertook to work out a framework in Washington for Cabinet level support of the Task Force idea. I went to talk to him about this on the afternoon of Foley's resignation. He was enthusiastic about what was being done in Oakland and hopeful that a way could be found to provide a counterpart in Washington for this interagency effort. I then urged that primary responsibility for dealing with each urban area be assigned to one department of the government, just as the State Department is responsible in each foreign country for bringing together the position of all agencies of the government as part of a coordinated United States policy. I also suggested that a high-level representative should be designated to speak for the entire government in each urban area, just as an ambassador does abroad. I pointed out that legislation providing such representatives to deal with groups of states was already in effect for the Appalachian Regional Commission and the Regional Action Planning Commissions then being set up under the Economic Development Act. The day before I made a similar suggestion to Secretary Connor; he liked the idea and suggested that it might be desirable to create a new "Department of Internal Affairs" for this purpose.

During October, the Critical Urban Affairs Steering Committee met twice with Mayor Reading, City Manager Keithley, and the heads of all the city departments concerned with Federal programs, to begin to plan for a coordinated approach.

As a result of these meetings, Mayor Reading decided to make a hurried trip to Washington early in November, to try to expedite two urban development projects which were of particular importance then because prospective tenants—a large department store, a convention hotel, and a community college—would be lost to downtown Oakland if approval was not obtained quickly. I was in Washington then, and urged John Macy to use Reading's presence there as the occasion for a joint meeting of all agencies involved in Oakland, to review developments and consider the Task Force recommendation. The meeting was held on the afternoon of November 9, the day after Election Day, in the offices of the Department of Housing and Urban Development. We spent nearly two hours reviewing the Oakland situation in detail and considering the potential of the Task Force proposal. When some of the Washington officials had difficulty comprehending the need for coordinating Federal programs, Mayor Reading put his feeling bluntly: "Believe me, gentlemen, what we need in Oakland is a Federal czar, who can direct all these programs, and with whom we can deal directly."

This startled some of those present, especially the staff of the Department of Housing and Urban Development, which had been criticized by many Mayors for proposing a Federal Coordinator—with very limited powers—in the Demonstration Cities program, and the ones from the Poverty Program, whose community action councils were then being attacked by some Mayors for undermining the authority of city governments. No one responded directly to the Mayor's suggestion. They talked instead of "providing a focus in Washington" for the work of the Federal Executive Board's Steering Committee and Task Force, and of the need for "fitting the mechanism to the problem." At the end, Bob Wood, who was presiding, said, "Mayor Reading, this discussion has been very helpful to me, and I am sure I can say the same for the others here. I hope it has also been helpful to you."

Mayor Reading replied: "I wish I could say it has been helpful, but I have not obtained what I feel we need, which is a clear line of authority. I was confused when I came here, and I am still confused. But it does make me feel better to have learned that you are all just as confused as I am."

Chapter X

Nearly a Riot

ANNE GOULD, in her report on Oakland written a few weeks after the Watts riot, said:

While there are moderates in the Negro community who do not want violence, there are those, especially among the younger element, who do. To these latter, Watts is a symbol and slogan for action. One hears repeatedly from the younger people: "We need a Watts here. It's the only way to get action; it's the only way to make 'em listen. . . .

This was quoted, along with much else from her report, in a lead story in *The Wall Street Journal* on January 5, 1966, under a headline reading:

RACIAL TINDERBOX

A Federal Study Finds
Unrest Among Negroes
Rising in Many Cities

New Watts Type Rioting Is
Feared; Vietnam's Inroads
On Great Society a Factor

A Look at Oakland's Troubles

187

Ramparts Magazine, in a long report on Oakland, expressed similar fears. So did the *Los Angeles Times,* which found Oakland a welcome substitute for Watts as an example of ghetto problems, and several news magazines.

One day when Jerry Keithley, Oakland's city manager, was grumbling about all this unfavorable publicity, I told him I thought we were lucky to have it. If we had a riot, everyone would say it was inevitable; if we didn't, we would look like heroes.

All of this, however, led many to feel that EDA's purpose in coming to Oakland was to prevent a riot. This worried me. My feeling, frequently expressed, was: Our program is not aimed at riot prevention now, but at long-term elimination of one of the causes of the riots—joblessness.

I was trying to say that the success or failure of the EDA experiment should not be judged by whether or not there was a riot in Oakland in 1966, but I knew that I was whistling in the dark.

As the summer of 1966 progressed, there were riots in Chicago, Brooklyn, Cleveland, and Louisville. Thinking and reading about them, we realized that Oakland had one advantage over the ghettos of those cities, in that it had no "long, hot summer." Summers in the Bay Area are cool, much cooler than spring or fall, as the rising heat in California's hot Central Valley behind the coastal range draws in the cool Pacific fog. The days seldom rise above the low 70s, and the nights drop into the 50s. But the absence of hot nights was offset by the knowledge that conditions in the Oakland ghetto were deteriorating, and that neither jobs, housing, nor education were being improved.

During the summer, there were many rumors in the Oakland ghetto that Molotov cocktails were being manufactured in empty garages; that arms caches had been discovered; and that new tactics based on a study of Watts were being taught to young Negro militants, stressing the folly of burning their own homes and shops in the ghetto, and urging that their protest would be more effective if they burned City Hall, the business district, and the homes of the Whites on the hillside.

These rumors did not circulate widely, but we heard them often enough to keep us worried, and apprehensive at the sound of sirens in the night.

On August 17, I had just returned, delayed by the airline strike, from a hurried trip to Washington to help prepare a statement for Foley to use in testifying before a Congressional Committee which was considering the "Farbstein Amendment" to make EDA funds available in all large city ghettos. In this statement, we took the risk of emphasizing that Oakland, in spite of earlier predictions, had not had a riot that summer.

On arriving at the Boatel that evening, I found telephone messages from Bill Becker, Governor Brown's assistant for human relations, and from Hugh Taylor. When I reached Becker at his home, he told me that there was a report of a riot in Oakland. I said I knew nothing, but would check and call back. Taylor had called to try to locate me for Becker, and knew nothing except that there had been a police alert for some trouble in East Oakland.

I called Doug Costle, to ask him to try to locate Mark Comfort—fortunately just released from jail on an order from Supreme Court Justice Douglas—and to meet me at our office in Jack London Square. Then I reached Fred Scott, just assigned from the EDA Seattle office to work on Employment Plans, and Ed O'Connell, of the Justice Department's Community Relations Service. O'Connell had already been alerted and was gathering facts. We agreed to meet in the EDA office to pool our information.

My idea was that we might be helpful, with the direct contacts all of us had in the ghetto, by piecing together an accurate story of what had happened and what was happening, to keep others informed and to alert anyone who should be involved.

189

Calls to the Mayor's and City Manager's offices confirmed that both were out of town at meetings, and could not be reached. This increased the need for coordination.

From experience in wildcat strikes, which were frequent in the New York newspaper industry, and from reading about the Watts and Harlem riots, I knew that one of the greatest dangers in any such fast moving crisis is the way rumors spread, become accepted as fact, and lead to action far different from that required by the real situation.

When Costle, Scott, and O'Connell arrived, I warned them of the need to check every report they heard from anyone not an eyewitness and to assume that every secondhand report was exaggerated until they had verified it from an independent source closer to the event. We manned our three phone lines and got busy.

Gloria Comfort, Mark's wife, told Doug Costle that her husband was already out in the streets, but was phoning in to keep her and others posted. Doug then called Evan Golder, of the West Oakland Parish, who was getting calls from those on the scene. His information proved to be more accurate than most.

Fred Scott, who as a Negro felt he would be safer there than any of the rest of us, left to report by phone from the scene. He warned us to stay off the streets if the trouble spread, saying, "No White man was safe in Watts." Also, he urged me to move into the back office, away from the big glass window looking out on First Street. Perhaps foolishly, I decided to stay at my own desk.

Ed O'Connell established contact with the Police Department, and then with those he knew in the ghetto.

My first call was to the East Oakland Parish, whose headquarters was near the scene of the reported trouble, on East 14th Street. John Frykman was en route from his home, and I found the minister in charge, a highly emotional person, in a state bordering on panic. His report was that a Negro girl

190

had been manhandled by the police during an arrest, and that this had set off an attack by hundreds of young Negroes, who were engaged in a pitched battle with the police. He said dozens of rioters were being taken off by ambulance to a nearby hospital. None of this proved to be true, fortunately. He had put it together from stories coming in from the streets and had not observed any of it himself.

Disregarding my own advice, I ended my report to the others dramatically: "Well, I guess Oakland's had it." Doug Costle intervened, and said that, while his first report from Mark Comfort had been pessimistic, a later one from Evan Golder indicated that the first rumors, which I had just heard repeated, were wildly exaggerated.

As we sorted out fact from fiction, it quickly became apparent that an isolated incident had promptly been brought under control. A group of youngsters had broken some store windows on East 14th Street. When the police arrived, a large crowd gathered, and moved into a construction lot nearby to pick up bricks and pieces of wood. More police came and dispersed the crowd, chasing some of them down side streets. There was no shooting, but a number of arrests were made. There were no serious injuries. There was some criticism by ghetto leaders of what they felt to be an excessive show of force by the police, who came in special riot cars, each carrying five men, equipped with crash helmets, riot batons, and shotguns. In spite of this criticism, they expressed relief at the speed with which the outbreak was put down.

It was all over before midnight. I called Bill Becker to report, and we went home. On the way, a few blocks up Broadway, Doug Costle passed two police cars. The police were frisking a heavily armed group of older Negroes, who had apparently come in off the Freeway looking for trouble.

The police maintained a heavy patrol in the East Oakland area all that night, but there were no further incidents.

Mark Comfort spent most of the night on the streets in

East Oakland, talking to the young Negroes who had been involved, and others who might be, calming them down, and sending them home. No one asked Mark to do this. He just did it, more effectively than anyone else in Oakland could have done. And he did it at considerable personal risk, since he had a "record," was just out of prison, and could easily have been picked up by the police for inciting the rioters, without their knowing that he was doing just the opposite.

We learned later that Mayor Reading returned to the city after midnight, heard what had happened, got in his little sports car, alone, with the top down, and toured the area where the trouble had been. Foolhardy, but admirable.

Months later, a report of the Oakland Police Department to the City Council revealed that, immediately after this incident, police officials met behind the scenes with Negro teenage leaders to discuss rumors of police brutality and rumors of plans for further violence, and felt that these talks helped to improve the atmosphere.

This incident occurred just a week before Mayor Reading was to testify at the Ribicoff subcommittee in Washington. Curtis Baker heard about it and called Jim Price, the Mayor's assistant to say he had some ideas for the Mayor to use. (I learned of this because I had the same idea, at the same time.) Price welcomed the suggestion and asked Baker to put his thoughts in writing and bring them in.

At the same time, Baker decided to do some riot prevention of his own, as the brief outbreak in East Oakland had had some repercussions among the younger hotheads in West Oakland. With the help of the West Oakland Parish mimeograph machine, he prepared and circulated a one-page handbill, which was crudely handlettered across the top:

NO-ONE FOR RIOTING IN
WEST OAKLAND

It was typed all in capitals, like a telegram, and read:

192

POOR PEOPLE OF WEST OAKLAND,
YOUNG AND OLD, THIS IS FROM CURTIS LEE BAKER.
I AM FOR HELPING OUR CAUSE. BUT WE BELIEVE ME
WE DONT HAVE TO RIOT BECAUSE THE MAYOR OF
OAKLAND. THIS MAN ASURE ME THAT HE IS DOING
SOMTHING FOR US. HE IS GOING TO WASHINGTON. D.C.
TO DEMAND HELP FOR MORE JOBS. THIS IS BETTER
THEN OUR PASS MAYOR DID.

NOW WE HAVE SOMTHING TO WAIT ON, I DON'T GIVE
A DAM A BOUT WHAT OTHER PEOPLE IN OTHER AREAS
ARE SAYING AND DOING. WE MIGHT STOP AND THINK
THAT PEOPLE ARE TRYING TO MAKE US BE KILLED.
I KNOW MANY PEOPLE WILL CRY I AM ON THE POWER
SIDES. I AM LOOKING OUT FOR THE POOR PEOPLES OF
THIS WEST OAKLAND. THE MAYOR IS USING MY RE-
PORT TO WORK WITH,

I CAN SAY EVERYTHING I HAVE TOLD THE MAYOR
THAT IS WHO IS BEHIND THE POOR PEOPLE SUFFER-
ING. WHAT AND WHY THE POOR PEOPLE COULD NOT
GET JOBS, HE CAME OUT WITH A FULL PUBLIC RE-
PORT AND I KNOW MANY DOORS ARE BEING OPEN
NOW AND BLACK PEOPLE ARE GETTING JOBS. I AM A
TRUE LEADER AND I WANTS WHAT IS BEST FOR MY
PEOPLE, I DAM SURE DONT WONT TO SEE THEM
KILLED. I AM NOT PUTTING THIS OUT UNDER PRES-
SURE. I NOT AFRAID OF DIEING OR THE POWER. BUT
IF WE LET A HAND FULL OF PEOPLE GET SOMONE
HURT AND KILLED WE ARE FOOLS,

I AM ONE OF THE MAYOR PUBLIC RELATION. I AM NOT
SAYING HE CAN DO EVERYTHING HE SAYS BUT THE
PEOPLE OF WEST OAKLAND AND OTHER AREAS
SHOULD GIVE HIM A CHANCE TO DO GOOD OR BAD, I
AM BACKING THE MAYOR PROGRAMS, IF YOU ARE
FOR RIGHT AND EQUAL FREEDOM YOU WILL ALLOW
HIM TO PUT HIS PROGRAMS IN ACTION, I AM NOT BE-
HIND ANY DAM RIOT NOR AM I FOR ANYONE LEAD-

ING ME OR MY PEOPLE INTO WAR BECAUSE THEY
FEEL LEFT OUT, BECAUSE SEEMS EVERYWHERE ELSE
IS RIOTING AND WE ARE NOT.

PEOPLE ARE TRYING TO GET US TO HELP THEM, I
WILL DIE FIRST BEFORE I LET ANYONE LEAD MY
PEOPLE TO THEIR DEATH. DEATH IS NOT WHAT I
WANTS FOR MY PEOPLE. DO NOT BE APART OF SO
CALL LEADERS (B, S) THESE PEOPLE CAN NOT DO
NOTHING FOR US, WE MUST WORK WITH GOOD TRUE
LEADERS. I KNOW THE WEST OAKLAND SERVICE CEN-
TER IS PUTING OUT I AM PART OF THE RIOTING IN
OTHER AREAS. THAT IS A LIE. ANYONE WHO IN ANY-
WAY SAYS THAT IS A LIE. SO DONT BE MADE TO DO
SOMTHING THAT EACH OF US WILL BE SORRY OF
LATER ON. I WILL BE AT MY OFFICE YOU CAN CALL
ME, LETS PUT THIS DAM MESS DOWN.

It would be hard to find a better example of the value of
the Mayor's "open-door" policy. As I read this in the Mayor's
anteroom, I thought of Curtis Baker's greeting to us in the
previous December, when he threatened, if the Negroes didn't
get "justice now ... we'll have a Watts here, and kill and
bomb."

The Mayor's testimony in Washington and the publicity
about the Job Fair, which was held in September, all had a
good effect in the Oakland ghetto.

Across the Bay, in the Hunters Point ghetto of San Francisco, serious riots occurred early in October. The Critical
Urban Problems Steering Committee was directed by the
White House staff to make recommendations for immediate
action in Hunters Point, and it quickly recommended that
more Federal jobs be opened up to young Negroes, and that
the community action program be expanded. These ideas met
with a negative response in Washington, however, partly because of a feeling that if the Federal government were to
move in with a crash program in response to a riot, this would

194

encourage more riots elsewhere. The rising tide of riots which swept across the country in the following year provided ample proof, if proof was needed, of the futility of this approach.

In the middle of October, when it began to look as if Oakland would get through 1966, at least, without serious trouble, a situation developed which seemed almost certain to bring it on. From the time of our first visits to the Oakland ghetto, we had heard frequent complaints about the schools and about the conservative attitude of the Oakland School Board. Earlier in the year, an "Ad Hoc Committee" of parents in the ghetto schools had been formed to negotiate with the School Board. It had presented a number of demands and met with a negative response. Toward the end of the summer, the Ad Hoc Committee declared that if the Board did not agree to meet its principal demands, a school boycott would be called on October 18, and that high-school students would not attend the regular schools.

Many of the high-school teachers were sympathetic with these demands, and cooperated with the Ad Hoc Committee in arranging to set up "Freedom Schools" which the boycotting students would attend from October 18–21. The idea was that students attending the Freedom Schools would not be truants, and would not be subject to discipline for not attending the regular schools. They lined up a number of church recreation halls, neighborhood centers, and other buildings for this purpose.

The threat of the boycott had no impact on the School Board except to stiffen its attitude. Teachers were forbidden to teach in the Freedom Schools. The District Attorney of Alameda County threatened to prosecute any teacher who taught in a Freedom School for impairing the morals of minors. Many of the churches which had offered recreation halls for their use were persuaded at the last minute to withdraw them.

The Ad Hoc Committee was just not equipped to cope with

195

this kind of opposition. While its aims were good, its leadership was ineffective. It lacked the ability to organize, even to provide adequate transportation to the few Freedom Schools that were able to operate. All that they succeeded in doing was to persuade most of the high-school students in the ghetto schools to stay out of school.

The result was that on Tuesday, October 18, several thousand high-school students were out on the streets with nothing to do, looking for trouble. They began to form large groups and roamed up and down East 14th Street, the main thoroughfare of East Oakland, breaking store windows and shouting at passers-by. The police were ready and turned out in force. Holding their clubs ahead of them with a hand over each end, they formed a solid wedge and cleared 14th Street, pushing the students ahead of them.

This was done with discipline and restraint and continued for four days. There were no serious injuries, and the relatively few arrests were apparently limited to those caught breaking windows or attacking the police. The action all took place during the day. An early curfew was imposed, and most parents kept their children off the streets at night.

The one serious incident occurred at the McClymonds High School, where the boycott had not been effective, and most students were attending classes. A large group broke in from the streets, disrupted several classes, beat up the teachers who opposed them, and overturned desks and other furniture. The police cordoned off the area, made a number of arrests, and restored order quickly.

On the evening of the second day, Wednesday, October 19, I went to a meeting of the Ad Hoc Committee that was reviewing the situation. Many responsible leaders like Don Mc-Cullum had, I knew, been trying, without success, during the day to persuade those heading the committee to call off the boycott. A few who raised this question at the meeting were ridiculed from the platform and attracted no support in the audience. The main discussion at the meeting was about what could be done to improve the Freedom School operations and to provide better transportation to them.

As this meeting broke up, Ed O'Connell and I talked on the sidewalk with Elijah Turner and Mark Comfort, who had been out for two days urging the high-school students to go home and stay out of trouble. To avoid conflict with the police, they had each teamed up with a White minister from the East Oakland Parish, whose clerical collar provided safe conduct. They said, however, that they had been refused permission to go through the police lines around the McClymonds High School that morning during the trouble there, and they urged Ed O'Connell to use his influence with the Police Department to get them through if anything like this happened again.

Throughout these four days, the police action on 14th Street received much coverage on local and national TV news programs, which created the impression that the situation was much worse than it really was. As I watched these programs, comparing what they showed with what I knew was happening from accurate on-the-spot reports, I realized two things about TV news coverage of urban riots which were a cause for concern.

First, the brief time allotted to any event on a TV news program almost guarantees that the most violent scenes are all that is displayed, and the viewer is thus led to assume that this violence is much more widespread than is actually the case. The newspaper accounts gave a much better balanced picture, because they covered much more of what happened, including the fact that order was quickly and firmly restored, while the TV screen showed only the more violent clashes between the police and the students. The local TV news was better than the national networks on this, because they gave more time to it. I learned also that the local TV reporters get paid more for items that are carried by the national networks, and are therefore likely to select the most sensational sequences for them.

197

In both cases, this selective reporting greatly exaggerated the amount of trouble, and the repetition of the more sensational shots on several successive programs during the day, when nothing new was happening, gave the impression that such things were continuing when they were not.

Second, the presence of the TV trucks, topped by their conspicuous camera turrets, moving slowly along behind the police lines, had a visible effect on the students being driven ahead of the line. They would make faces and shout things at the cameras, hoping to be seen by their friends. On one occasion an attractive Negro girl of about nineteen turned in front of the police line, looked up to make sure the camera was on her, shouted some insults at the police, and attacked one of them in a way that made sure she was wrestled to the ground, kicking and fighting. On another occasion, a boy looked up at the camera, turned, and tried to break back through the edge of the line, getting himself thrown down and arrested. Neither of these moves made any sense in the circumstances, except as a way of providing violent action for the cameras. In this they succeeded, and each of these sequences received a big play on all programs.

Things quieted down somewhat on Thursday and Friday, as parents seemed to be keeping their children home, off the streets and away from school, and there were no further serious incidents.

On Saturday, I began a report to Ross Davis, Foley's successor, which I had been preparing to urge prompt action on a number of pending projects, with these comments:

ACTION FOR OAKLAND
Recent events here in Oakland have illuminated the impact of the EDA program, and the need for further prompt action by EDA and other Federal agencies.

For the last four afternoons and evenings, bands of young Negroes, aroused and released by an ill considered and badly managed school boycott, have roamed up and down 14th Street in East Oakland, breaking store windows and throwing a few ineffective "Molotov cocktails." The police have responded firmly, in adequate numbers, without excess, and have kept the situation under effective control.

A year ago, when most close observers agreed that Oakland was ripe for a Watts explosion, it seems certain that a series of incidents like those of the past few days would have escalated into one. What has made the difference? One thing we know: The most militant young Negroes, who ten months ago were saying it would take a Watts to get anything done, were out in the streets sending kids home saying, "This is not the way to do it. Things are coming our way. We don't need a Watts here. It will be bad for us."

The fulcrum for this change was, I believe, provided by the EDA presence in Oakland from the Dunsmuir House announcement January 29 of the selection of Oakland for a $15,000,000 pilot project until the announcement April 29 of the $23,000,000 funded project. . . .

By April, 1966, the situation had visibly improved. The new Mayor, John Reading, had just taken office, and immediately accepted the major premise of our program, the need to solve the problems of unemployment by providing jobs as his main goal. The announcement of our funded projects at the end of April gave him a good solid platform from which to launch his own efforts to mobilize the business community. He has taken full advantage of this, and we have worked closely and effectively with him. His activities have convinced the ghetto residents that he is trying, and that he cares about solving their problems. This had made all the difference.

So, while the EDA program has not yet placed anyone in a job, and will not for many months, I believe that it did provide the real turning point for change in Oakland.

If the above analysis is correct, then it becomes doubly important to reinforce this favorable turn by immediately visible Federal action to provide jobs now for minorities. We have succeeded in raising hope in the ghetto. Failure to respond with action will cause a reaction of justified anger and despair. The imminent cutback of Poverty Program funds and program will also have this effect unless offset by other Federal action.

That was where things stood at the end of 1966.

The Report of the National Advisory Commission on Civil Disorders, released in February, 1968, begins: "The summer of 1967 brought racial disorder again to American cities, deepening the bitter residue of fear and threatening the future of all Americans." That report describes eight "major disorders" in 1967, and thirty-three "serious disorders." While none of these occurred in Oakland, the description of many of the cities in which they did occur is an accurate summary of what we found in Oakland in January, 1966. It also lists one hundred and twenty-three "minor disorders" which, it says, "would not have been classified as 'riots' or received wide press attention without national conditioning to a 'riot climate,'" since each lasted less than one day, caused little damage, and was handled by local police. One of these minor incidents occurred in Oakland.

Riots flared again in many city ghettos in April, 1968, after the murder of Martin Luther King. An incident in Oakland then, violent and serious, seemed likely to trigger a riot there —but this did not happen. It involved the Black Panthers, a militant group of young Negroes, which had become active in Oakland in 1967, operating patrols to follow police cars and to advise those arrested in the ghetto. The Black Panthers stressed self-defense and were armed for this. They favored militant political action, but were opposed to riots. On the night of April 6, two days after Dr. King's death, the Oakland police stopped a car full of Black Panthers. The reports of what followed are conflicting, but this much seems clear. Shooting started. Two policemen were shot. The Black Panthers ran from the car into a house. The police surrounded it. After a gun battle of over an hour, the Black Panthers surrendered. The first one to come out, eighteen-year-old Bobby Hutton, was shot and killed. Another, Eldridge Cleaver, author of *Soul on Ice,* was wounded.

The reaction in the Oakland ghetto was strong and angry. But, instead of violence, it took the form of organizing political and economic pressure for changes in the police department, such as hiring more Negro officers, more community control, walking policemen, abandoning heavy, warlike equipment, and indictment of the police who shot Hutton, which the grand jury, after a quick hearing, had not done. A "Blacks for Justice Committee" was formed, which started picketing stores, urging a boycott until merchants brought pressure on the police. Mayor Reading decried these "blackmail methods." The *Oakland Tribune* ran a full page advertisement calling the boycott attempt "coercion and extortion," with a picture of a gloved hand aiming a pistol out at the reader, asking: "What would you do in a case like this?" A Negro reporter on the *Tribune* said the ad amounted to "inciting a riot" and resigned. So did a White editor, who called it "an open invitation to violence."

The fact remains that Oakland, to its great credit, came through 1966, 1967, and the first half of 1968 without a serious riot. But, like all our cities, it will remain in precarious balance, on the edge of violence, until far more than is now in view can be done to improve life for those who dwell in the ghetto.

Chapter XI

The Lesson of Oakland

WHAT can be learned from the story of Oakland in 1966?

Reduced to its simplest terms, that story is:

As the year opened, we saw a deadlock between opposing forces.

On one side were the forces of protest and change—the residents of the Flatlands ghettos, in need of jobs, housing, schools, a better life. The Poverty Program, the new civil rights laws, the booming economy with its promise of good jobs for all, had raised high hopes that the better life was within reach, but few had found it. New leaders, the young Negro militants, the White ministers of the Flatlands parishes, the middle-class Negroes who were taking a more militant stand, all provided strong voices calling for change. The fires of Watts were a beacon to some, illuminating action within their reach if other means proved too slow. Others knew that the bitter aftermath of a riot would delay needed change, but wondered how enough could be done in time to avoid one. The growing success of the Delano strike had shown the Mexican-Americans that they too could organize and be heard. Throughout the country the climate favored protest—for civil rights in the South, against the Viet Nam war on college campuses.

On the other side were the forces of order and stability—the Mayor and the city administration, the businessmen, the labor unions—what the ghetto leaders like to call the "power structure." They were responsible for making the existing system function, for enforcing the laws, for keeping order. They had power, in the sense of the ability to run things as they were. But they did not have the power to provide the changes being demanded in the ghettos, because all of these—jobs, training, education, housing—required sums of money far beyond what city taxes could provide.

As the battle lines leading to this deadlock had been drawn, each side had become "the enemy" to the other. To the Mayor and most of the established community leaders, the "radicals" in the ghetto were the enemy because they were asking for things that could not be provided, and seemed to threaten chaos if their demands were not met. In fact, their very presence, and the numbers for whom they spoke, seemed to many to be a threat to Oakland's security and future growth. To the Flatlands residents, the so-called power structure and the White middle class were the enemy, because they possessed what was lacking in the ghetto—well-paid jobs, good houses, education, security—and seemed more interested in keeping these things for themselves than in helping others get them.

This deadlock was a dangerous one. Neither side could give the other what it wanted. On each side the leadership was divided and confused. Effective communication had broken down, and was being replaced by a growing exchange of epithets that both reflected and increased the lack of understanding between the two sides. In this atmosphere of suspicion and distrust, when the main contact between the ghetto and the establishment was through the police, it seemed inevitable that before long a police incident would provide the spark for a conflagration. When that came, the city government and the police would have to put it out, using whatever force this required. The outbreak of violence, and its repression by force, would solve no problems for either side, but only widen the gap between them.

In all this, Oakland had much in common with many other cities—more than most people realized, because the spotlight was on Oakland. Stories in publications as diverse as *Ramparts* and *The Wall Street Journal* had made Oakland a symbol of this dangerous urban confrontation.

Since then, so many of the other cities have exploded with serious riots that it is clear we face a national crisis of major proportions. But all through 1966, 1967, and the first half of 1968 Oakland has not suffered a riot.

We must then ask: What happened in Oakland that saved it from burning, when most observers thought it would be one of the first to go?

There are no easy answers to that question.

It may even be said that the question itself is irrelevant. All through the year 1966, I maintained that EDA's purpose in Oakland was not the prevention of a riot. Our purpose, instead, was to attack one of the main sources of frustration and despair in the ghetto—the inability to get jobs. Since this would take years of concentrated effort, I urged that the success or failure of the EDA program should not be judged by whether or not there was a riot.

Nevertheless, the fact that there was no riot in Oakland during those years cannot be ignored, as the country inquires into the causes of the riots elsewhere, and seeks to decide on the action needed to prevent them in the future.

Two events in Oakland during 1966 which may have made the difference can be identified.* The first was the dramatic,

* These directly affected two of the four characteristics of the "background of disorder in riot cities" identified in the *Report of the National Advisory Commission on Civil Disorders,* released in February, 1968. The two affected are italicized in the following quotation:
"The background of disorder in the riot cities was typically characterized

massive EDA program, directed at the central ghetto need, training and jobs. This was an experimental pilot project, something that was not being done on this scale or in this way in any other city. It was carried out with unusual speed, and was more fully coordinated with all related Federal, state, and city efforts than is usually the case with a large Federal program. The second was the local response to this new Federal approach. Following the change in the city administration, the new Mayor, John Reading, and the new City Manager, Jerome Keithley, succeeded in mobilizing first the business community, and then Minority groups and labor, to respond with effective local action. This supported the Federal job development and training programs with a broad local initiative along the same lines. It also provided more active local leadership to help solve the local problems of other Federal programs, by strengthening the community action machinery of the poverty program, expediting housing and urban renewal applications, and supporting the efforts to end discrimination in employment.

This increasingly effective combination of Federal and local action gradually dissolved the deadlock between the ghetto and the establishment. The Federal government, by paying for EDA job development and for training, provided money that was not available locally. The active cooperation of city officials, businessmen, and labor leaders in working out these programs put them on the side of those helping to make the changes needed to solve the basic ghetto problems of jobs and training. Once this commitment was demonstrated, the barriers of suspicion and distrust began to fall. It then became possible for the leaders of the ghetto Minorities to work with

---

by severely disadvantaged conditions for Negroes, especially as compared with those for whites; *a local government often unresponsive to these conditions; federal programs which had not yet reached a significantly large proportion of those in need;* and the resulting reservoir of pervasive and deep grievance and frustration in the ghetto." (Bantam Books edition, March, 1968, page 112.)

them on a basis of growing mutual respect and understanding.

Breaking the deadlock was a necessary first step, and may have saved Oakland from going the way of Newark, which it resembles in many ways. But the riots in Detroit and New Haven in the summer of 1967 make it clear that such a first step must be followed by many more. Each of those cities had developed strong local government and business support for substantial programs supported by Federal funds. These were regarded as models in the rest of the country, especially the Detroit Skills Center. Yet they had serious riots, Detroit's being the worst of any up to then.

Detroit and New Haven may offer this addition to the lesson of Oakland: The success of the first steps on the long road to the solution of ghetto problems raises new hopes and expectations; if these are not soon satisfied by continued and expanded programs, the disappointments that will follow can create a situation just as bad as the original deadlock. The frequently quoted warning of Kenneth B. Clark in his book *Dark Ghetto* has a direct bearing here:

It would not be realistic for the white community to expect protest to subside in the face of gains, for the closer the Negro community gets to the attainment of its goals—the removal of the causes and effects of racial exploitation and powerlessness—the more impatient will Negroes become for total equality.

In the complex turbulence of the Negro ghetto . . . success feeds hope and provides the strength and the motivation for further activity. This, in turn, makes existing barriers even more intolerable. . . .

If we accept this, as I believe we must, then two conclusions follow: *First,* as we have seen in Oakland, the dangerous deadlock between unmet ghetto needs and city power structures that lack the financial power to satisfy these needs can be broken by a successful combination of Federal funding and local community action. *Second,* this first step must be followed promptly by more effective Federal programs and more effective local response, until the needs are met and the barriers removed.

This is a large order. The Oakland experience throws some light on what may be required, at both the Federal and local levels. Of the three most important requirements in terms of new or expanded Federal programs, two are long range—the creation of new employment opportunities and the provision of the training needed to qualify for these. The third is the need for immediate shorter-range employment to cover the period before the long-range programs take effect. These three will be discussed in the remainder of this chapter. A separate and equally important requirement, adequate Federal and local administrative machinery to handle these and other large urban programs, will be treated separately in the next chapter. The three are:

First, the foremost ghetto need is more jobs—steady, well-paid jobs with prospects of advancement. To provide these:

• The EDA program of encouraging business expansion in or near areas of high unemployment, through a combination of public works, business loans, and planning grants—now available in only a handful of cities because of unrealistic statutory restrictions—should be extended to all cities. Several amendments to accomplish this have been held up in Congressional committees for over two years, mainly for budgetary reasons.

• New and more effective ways of encouraging business to locate or expand near ghetto areas should be added, such as interest rebates (deleted by Congress from the original EDA bill), tax incentives, insurance guaranties (a real problem after the claims from the 1967 riots), and whatever else seems likely to offer promise. Experimentation and the encouragement of local initiative should be the watchwords here, instead of the caution and delay that have been characteristic of both the Administration and Congress in recent years.

• If, as recent trends indicate, much industrial expansion is more feasible in the suburbs than in the central cities, ways must be found to provide low-cost housing in the suburbs near the new factories and to enable ghetto residents to occupy this housing.

• Artificial barriers to employment of ghetto residents, whether these stem from discrimination by employers or by unions, from unrealistic job qualifications concerning education or criminal records, or from union hiring practices, must be eliminated. Compared to the real barrier, the lack of education and training, these probably are today a small part of the total problem. Most of them are already banned by Federal and state laws. But where these laws are not enforced— so conspicuously in the building trades and in some municipal employment—the symbolic effect of the violations is severe.

Second, adequate training is the essential bridge between the unskilled ghetto residents and most job openings. To provide this:

• The existing training programs of MDTA and the Poverty Program should be expanded to absorb all who need them, not just the small percentages now being served. The complex administrative systems of each, especially of MDTA with its division of responsibility between so many Federal and state agencies, need to be streamlined to eliminate the present delays and confusion.

• New ways must be found to relate training to prospective employment, with less reliance on the negative traditions of joint employer-union apprentice programs. More effective use can be made of long-range forecasts of changes in the labor market, adapted to local conditions through better communication with local employers.

• Better means must be found of reaching and recruiting the hard-core unemployed, both young and old, who are now reluctant to enter the labor market or the training programs. For them also, new techniques of motivational training are needed, to enable them to believe that there is a chance for them to succeed. The techniques developed by ghetto residents themselves in the OIC programs initiated by Reverend Leon Sullivan in Philadelphia and elsewhere have great promise here.

Third, immediate employment should be provided by the Federal government, as the employer of last resort, for all who cannot qualify for openings in the normal labor market. The considerations leading to this drastic, costly conclusion are:

• Many years must pass before training programs and economic development on the scale proposed here can provide full employment to those in the city ghettos who need it so desperately now—or to the rural unemployed who are continuing to move into the cities. For example, the first steps taken in Oakland in 1966—the $30 million committed by EDA then would be $7 billion on a national scale—should provide jobs for about one fifth of Oakland's unemployed over a period of several years. This means that, even if these programs are expanded at the same level every two years, it will be ten years before Oakland's present unemployment problem is resolved, without taking into account new entries into the labor market.

• Therefore, immediate action of an interim nature seems imperative, to arrest the further deterioration of our central cities, now accelerating at a rate which soon will render long-range solutions futile.

• For this purpose, providing employment for all who can work seems preferable to such alternatives as the "negative income tax" or expanded welfare payments, as those would merely underwrite the continued inactivity of those now unable to achieve their place in society by earning their own living.

• The experience of the WPA and the CCC in the thirties, from which we are now reaping rewards in recreation areas,

209

reforestation and the TVA, shows that much work of lasting social benefit can be found for such an emergency employment program. Today, urban renewal, cleaning out the automobile graveyards that blight the countryside, and reforesting vast timbered-out and mined-out areas are projects that come quickly to mind. More careful study will reveal many more, especially among things which can be done to improve the environment in our run-down, dirty, older cities.

• As part of such employment, almost all of which will initially have to be at an unskilled level, extensive on-the-job training can be provided, first to equip the trainees for higher-skilled and supervisory jobs within the program, and then eventually for jobs outside in business and industry.

These represent, in my judgment, the programs now most urgently needed in our cities, based on my observation of the problems of one city, Oakland, in the year 1966. The events of 1967 in many other cities have led other observers to similar conclusions. The emphasis here on programs related to employment is not, however, intended to suggest that they should be expanded at the expense of other programs vitally needed in the ghettos—housing and urban renewal, community action, and health, education, and welfare. All of these need to be continued, improved, and expanded to provide a concerted attack on the total problem of the urban ghetto.

A massive application of Federal funds will be required to accomplish all of this. Estimates of the amount needed have covered a broad range, expressed in terms of multiples of $10 billion per year. A realistic figure to cover what is proposed here is something in the neighborhood of $30 billion annually.

So far, the answer of the Administration and of Congress to all proposals of this magnitude has been that we cannot afford them while we are spending $30 billion annually in Viet Nam. This sounds, on the surface, like budgetary prudence, until one stops to think what it really means. This is, that the price we have chosen to pay for continuing the Viet Nam war has been the further degradation of the lives of those who dwell in our urban ghettos, the group in our society least able to bear this burden. This choice also rests on the questionable assumption that the future security of the nation depends more on solving the Viet Nam problem than on solving the problems of our cities.

Surely, even if we accept the basic idea that we cannot afford to increase the total national budget by an amount sufficient to meet pressing urban needs, there are two other choices open to us within this framework which deserve equally thoughtful consideration: *Either*, we can end the Viet Nam war and devote the sums needed to resolving the urban crisis; *Or*, we can divert other resources—through increased taxation and by deferring such luxuries as the space program and the development of the supersonic airliner—to meet the more immediate needs of the cities.

I must confess, however, that I fail to understand the economic reasoning that leads to the belief that we cannot afford these big urban programs unless the government curtails other spending. My difficulty is this: The expenditure of $30 billion per year in Viet Nam, now a major stimulant to our economy, provides employment for, one may assume, about as many people as would be employed if the same amount were being spent for some other purpose. If that is so, then when the war ends, as it someday must, an equivalent expenditure—whether by government or by individuals and businesses after a tax reduction—will be needed just to provide new employment for those laid off after the cut in military spending. This will leave the problem of unemployment in the ghettos just where it is today—unresolved.

However that may be, it probably doesn't matter. What we are talking about is adding some $25 billion to the $5 to $7 billion now being spent on programs related to the problems of urban poverty and unemployment. Twenty-five billion dollars is 3 percent of our gross national product, now passing $800 billion. This is half its annual rate of growth, 6 percent in current dollars, for the last ten years. Surely the most affluent nation in the world can afford to allocate, in one way or another, that much of its resources to secure a better future for all its residents, as it did successfully in the depression of the thirties and in World War II.

My proposition is a very simple one: We cannot afford *not* to spend what is required to solve the problems of the ghettos, because the failure to solve them is endangering the future of our cities, the centers of growth and strength in our increasingly urban society. And even if, as some propose, we could contain this danger through repressive police action and limited welfare palliatives, this would merely postpone the day of reckoning. As a nation committed from the beginning to the principles of equality and opportunity, we could not for long continue to deny both of these to the large segment of our urban citizens now prevented from attaining them by historical and economic forces beyond their control.

I am convinced that the country will provide the many billions needed to solve its urban problems—perhaps not as soon as it should, which will mean that the cost will be greater than if the action were prompt—but soon enough to get the job done, as it always has in the past when faced with comparable threats to its future.

This chapter, up to this point, had been written in October, 1967, four months before the publication of the Report of the National Advisory Commission on Civil Disorders. Chapter 16 of that Report, *The Future of the Cities,* and Chapter 17, *Recommendations for National Action,* present the Commission's conclusions, based on an extensive study and analysis of the principal cities where riots occurred in 1967. These represent the most advanced, and in my view the wisest, thinking that has appeared in this difficult field. After reading them, my first impulse was to drop this chapter, and simply state my

212

full agreement with the Commission's conclusions. I have decided to keep it as it was written, however, as an independent supporting comment on their report, coming from study of a city that did not riot, and was therefore outside the scope of their inquiry.

The comprehensive and penetrating conclusions in Chapters 16 and 17 of the Commission's Report include specific recommendations about the content of the programs needed to attain their stated goals in the fields of employment, education, welfare, and housing. They do not, however, make any recommendation for the administrative machinery that will be needed to handle these vast new programs, though the need for this is clearly stated:

Yet there is little doubt that the system through which federal programs are translated into services to people is a major problem in itself. There are now over 400 grant programs operated by a broad range of federal agencies and channeled through a much larger array of semi-autonomous state and local government entities. Reflective of this complex scheme, federal programs often seem self-defeating and contradictory: field officials unable to make decisions on their own programs and unaware of related efforts; agencies unable or unwilling to work together; programs conceived and administered to achieve different and sometimes conflicting purposes.

The new social development legislation has put great strain upon obsolescent machinery and administrative practices at all levels of government. It has loaded new work on federal departments. It has required a level of skill, a sense of urgency, and a capacity for judgment never planned for or encouraged in departmental field offices. It has required planning and administrative capacity rarely seen in statehouses, county courthouses and city hall.

Deficiencies in all of these areas have frustrated accomplishment of many of the important goals set by the President and the Congress.

In recent years serious efforts have been made to improve program coordination. . . . Yet, despite these and other efforts, the Federal Government has not yet been able to join talent, funds and programs for concentrated impact in the field. Few agencies are able to put together a comprehensive package of related programs to meet priority needs.

There is a clear and compelling requirement for better coordination of federally funded programs, particularly those designed to benefit the residents of the inner city. If essential programs are to be preserved and expanded, this need must be met. (Bantam Books edition, March, 1968; pp 411-412; emphasis added.)

In the next chapter, some of the major questions arising from the administration of large Federal-city programs are examined, and a new, practicable mechanism, based on the Oakland experience, is proposed for dealing with them. These are important questions, since the failure to resolve them could seriously impair, and possibly destroy, the effectiveness of the larger programs now so badly needed.

Chapter XII

The Management of Big Federal-City Programs

AMERICANS have demonstrated again and again their capacity for successful innovation in the techniques of administering large enterprises—in giant industrial corporations, in big universities, and even in government.

This capacity, however, has not been much in evidence in the current debate over the growing urban crisis. Most of the discussion has been directed at the content of new programs, and at their cost, and very little at the equally important question of the administrative machinery that will be needed to make them work. There is wide agreement that the present machinery is inadequate, and that new ways must be found to plan, coordinate, and administer the large and growing urban programs now divided among so many Federal, state, and local agencies. Since they all depend to a large extent on Federal financial support, the method most readily available for this purpose is the control of the flow of Federal funds. In all these programs, the Federal agencies and the cities are inextricably joined, not by choice, but by necessity. They are, quite literally, opposite sides of the same coin.

As now organized, both suffer from divisions of responsibility which, while useful for many purposes, keep them from functioning effectively.

The Federal government, for reasons we will examine later, has approached the interlocking urban needs by setting up separate programs, administered by separate agencies, to handle economic development, training, fair employment, housing, urban renewal, transportation, health, education, welfare, and community action. Each of these agencies operates by approving individual projects, usually in Washington, on the basis of national priorities. There is no adequate mechanism, either in Washington or in any urban area, for coordinating the efforts of all these agencies so that all the projects in any city and its region will form a consistent pattern.

In the urban regions, the conditions of poverty, unemployment, and their related ills are concentrated in the older central cities. Therefore, the programs aimed at their relief—welfare, health, education, housing, and community action—must also be concentrated there. But their causes, the failures in planning, in economic development, in transportation, and in land use choices, lie partly, at least, outside the older cities, in the suburbs. Programs designed to deal with these causes must, to succeed, involve both city and suburban governments. As yet, no adequate mechanism exists in any metropolitan region for bringing these separate governments together with those of the states and the nation for this purpose. The absence of such coordination has been an important cause of the failures which have concentrated poverty in the older cities.

Further, these divisions of responsibility are different in kind. For the Federal agencies, they are based on the nature of their programs, but for the urban regions, on the accidental geography of municipal boundaries. This difference compounds the difficulty of reconciling their attitudes, and even

216

makes it hard for them to define the nature of their joint administrative problem.

To the Mayor of Oakland, the most serious administrative problem is the need for better coordination of all the Federal programs available in Oakland. To the Federal administrator considering a project submitted from Oakland, one of the most serious questions is whether it is consistent with sound planning for the Bay Area and the nation. The Mayor is not, of course, unaware of the need for joint action between Oakland and other parts of the Bay Area. Nor does the Federal representative, especially when he is on the scene in Oakland, fail to see the need to coordinate what he is doing with other Federal programs. But to each, the mote in the other's eye is more visible than the beam in his own.

This may suggest the need of a joint solution, an administrative mechanism which can coordinate all Federal programs in each region in response to guidance from a group competent to speak for the region as a whole. Let us keep this possibility in mind as we review first the manner of growth of these metropolitan regions, and then the way in which the separate Federal programs have evolved.

In this process, it will be helpful to make a clear distinction between the useful functions which maintain the health of a region and the conditions of distress caused by the failure of any of these functions. Treating these conditions may be necessary, but they will not be cured until the malfunction has been corrected. Aspirin will relieve the headache, but it will not do the work of the antibiotic.

The urban pattern of the metropolitan region began to appear early in the twentieth century, evolved slowly until its growth was checked by the Great Depression and World War II, and has grown with explosive force during the last two decades. This is an extreme example of growth which creates tasks beyond the capacity of the existing administrative mechanisms. The nineteenth-century city, where this growth began,

217

was an urban island in a rural sea. As a political and administrative unit, it had the capacity—not always exercised—to control within its borders the urban functions of transportation, the regulation of land use, waste disposal, and even, so far as it was then recognized, planning and economic development. Almost all of these functions were carried out by the activities of private business in response to the demands of the market, but government could and did intervene when necessary.

As each urban area's growth flowed out beyond the original city's borders, the surrounding rural towns and counties became its suburbs, forming a metropolitan region, where some of these urban functions were required in response to regional needs. The separate municipal governments of city and suburb failed to create adequate administrative mechanisms for this purpose, though many of their limited efforts were partially successful. This left most of the task to the decisions of business and the market, which also failed in many ways to meet the region's needs.

The country's metropolitan regions show great diversity, caused by their differences in age, size, geography, and forms of economic growth, but some patterns of government are common to all. Each contains one or more older core cities, still the main centers of employment in business and in industry, where the problems of race and poverty became paramount as rural migrants replaced the White middle class. They are surrounded by expanding rings of suburban towns, cities, and counties. These are the homes of those who hold many of the better jobs in the core cities, as well as the increasing number of good jobs in the suburbs themselves. Several regions are divided by state boundaries as well as municipal ones. Each is united by an urban pattern built around the journey from home to work.

Within each region, there are many forms of local government. There are cities, towns, and counties. Their executives

218

include mayors, city managers, superintendents. Their legislative bodies vary widely in size and type, some bearing ancient titles—Freeholders, Selectmen, or Aldermen—others the modern designations of municipal reform. They exhibit different degrees of efficiency, of honesty, of responsiveness to the needs of their citizens. Most of them are units of manageable size in relation to the services which they provide through local taxes: police and fire protection; education through high school and sometimes beyond; streets that are paved and lighted; water and sewer systems; parks and museums; and the other amenities of city and suburban life.

The ability of the local governments to provide these services should be protected and strengthened. Where imbalances exist between local governments in their ability to cover the cost of these services through local taxes, state and county action to equalize tax distribution is needed. This is most evident in the case of educational costs in high poverty areas. Much has been done to equalize these imbalances, and more will be needed. When this is not done, the resistance of local governments to regional decisions about the location of industry and housing is greatly increased.

These services provided by the local governments are of great importance to the region as a whole, since they determine much of the quality of urban life. The metropolitan region, however, is more than the sum of these parts. It is bound together by certain major functions, already mentioned, which are regional, not local, in character. These exceed the capacity of the individual local governments, and cannot be successfully performed unless regional mechanisms are created to bring together the local, state, and Federal governments for this purpose. A brief analysis of each of these functions should suffice to show why this is the case:

Planning: The close interrelationships between these regional functions require that they be planned together on a regional basis, so that all decisions about them can be made consistently in a manner best suited to the region's needs. This is now well recognized, but it was a novelty as recently as 1929, when a group of private citizens, not a government body, completed the "Regional Plan of New York and its Environs." The Second Regional Plan for the enlarged metropolitan region is now being constructed by the Regional Plan Association. Few comparable plans exist for other metropolitan regions, though many are now in preparation.

The unplanned growth of every metropolitan region, including much of the New York area not affected by its planning, is the principal reason for the conditions of distress now so evident in them. As the Federal government in the last decade has become increasingly involved in the problems of the metropolitan regions, it has begun to require regional planning as a condition of most large Federal grants, and has made many different forms of planning grants available. So have many states, and they, through their planning agencies, have done much of the needed work. In spite of all this, much remains to be done before any metropolitan region will have a planning mechanism adequate to the task of continuous planning for the region's future.

Economic Development: The malfunction which is the principal cause of the condition of poverty and unemployment is that of economic development. This term is used here in a broad sense to include the development not only of material resources, but also of human resources, through the elimination of such barriers to employment as discrimination, educational failures, and the lack of needed skills. There are, of course, also strong moral and social reasons for removing these barriers, but the action needed to remove them can be taken most effectively by those responsible for the entire function of economic development.

Economic development, the product of the combined efforts of government, business, and industry, is a national function as well as a regional one. The decisions and action which shape

220

it in one region affect its form in others. The form it has taken in rural areas in recent years, for example, the rapid mechanization of agriculture, mining and forestry, is one of the principal reasons for the migration of the unskilled rural unemployed to the cities. The new economic development programs for many of these rural areas may do much to arrest this migration in the future. They may even reverse it to some extent, as the recent rapid development of Puerto Rico has done, but this cannot be expected to relieve the present condition of urban unemployment to any great degree.

The reduction of urban unemployment will have to come mainly from economic development in the metropolitan regions, where recent patterns of growth indicate that much more is possible. These patterns within each region, however, indicate also that growth cannot be achieved by economic development in the cities alone, but only by development throughout the region.

While most of this development depends on individual business decisions, these can be strongly influenced by government action of various kinds, applied as part of a regional plan, such as port development and the location of rail lines, highways, and industrial parks. The EDA statute represents a direct attempt to influence these decisions in several ways, which could be made available throughout each metropolitan region. Decisions of the Federal government about the location of various facilities, post offices, office buildings, court houses, and military installations, and the disposal of surplus land, can have an important bearing here, as can state decisions on the location of hospitals, colleges, and other activities.

If this analysis is correct, the foremost task of the administrative mechanism we are seeking must be to accelerate the pace of economic development within each region to eliminate the condition of poverty and unemployment.

Control of land use patterns: Decisions as to the location and concentration of business, industry, housing of various types, parks, recreation, and other uses of the available land have had a profound effect on the way the different parts of each region have developed. Most of these decisions can be controlled by government action. Federal and state grants and subsidies for low- and middle-income housing involve decisions about its location. Far too much low-income housing has been concentrated by these programs in the older cities, partly because of its relation to slum clearance and because it was a municipal program. The FHA mortgage program has been a major factor in the rapidity of the exodus of the White middle class from the city to the suburbs. Zoning ordinances in the suburbs often permit only middle- and high-income development by limiting lots to one acre or more, creating the "spread city" of low density. The location of highways and rail lines, financed by both state and Federal governments, influences the location of housing, business, and industry.

The growing concentration of population in metropolitan regions, and the resulting shrinkage of open space available for recreation, has led to much action by the Federal, state, and local governments to provide parks and recreation areas, which have a direct and lasting effect on land use.

All of these forms of government action to control patterns of land use should be taken with more attention to their relationship to the needs of the metropolitan region as a whole.

Transportation: The provision of highways connecting the different parts of each region with each other and with other parts of the country has long been recognized as a responsibility of the Federal government and of the states. Ports and airports connecting the region with the nation and the world have been developed by various combinations of local, state, and Federal financing. Rail transportation, left in private hands and heavily taxed, suffered from the competition of the alternative forms of transportation supported by the government. As a result, much of it has been taken over by the government—by cities in the case of local subways and the buses

222

that have replaced the street cars, by cities, suburbs and states in the case of suburban commuter lines, and by the Federal government in the development of high-speed inter-city passenger service. Decisions about each of these forms of transportation have direct effects on the others, and also on other regional functions, such as economic development and land use.

A wide variety of public authorities have been set up to finance and operate all of these forms of transportation in each region. Too often these authorities, limited by the special purpose for which they were created, have made their decisions without sufficient regard for their effect on other forms of transportation and other regional functions.

Waste Disposal: The concentrations of population and industry in each metropolitan region require that the function of waste disposal be handled to a large extent on a regional basis and, in the case of contiguous regions sharing the same air currents, rivers, or lakes, on a state or national basis. Past failures in this regard have created conditions of air, water, and land pollution which are today regarded as a national problem and are the subject of combined Federal, state, and local programs.

The separation in this analysis of regional functions and of the conditions caused by their failure is an arbitrary one, and other classifications would serve as well. The important thing is to recognize that these functions must be planned and carried out, and these conditions remedied, in concert, not separately. As this is done, it will be helpful to distinguish between cause and effect, between malfunction and the resulting condition. In every case, the treatment for the latter provides needed temporary relief, but it does not reach the malfunction which is its cause. The form of the treatment, however, may make it more difficult to attack the cause, unless they are considered together.

The failure to make this distinction between cause and effect has caused some confusion in the approach to the condition of poverty and unemployment, concentrated in the central cities. Economic development, the only function which can eliminate this condition, should take place where the conditions for growth are most favorable. To the extent that these locations are outside the central cities, in the suburbs or elsewhere, some of the treatment, at least housing and education, should be located near the economic development. And one proposed treatment, the negative income tax, unless carefully designed, could seriously impede economic development by removing the incentive for training to fill new jobs.

The distinction between function and condition is of value for another reason. The planning and administration of the regional functions of economic development, controlling land use, transportation, and waste disposal, are constructive, creative acts, in which the different governments and private interests involved can be expected to join with some enthusiasm. This is not the case with the conditions caused by the failure of these functions, which are more likely to be avoided by those not directly affected by them.

It makes little sense to the resident of a suburb to say, "For the good of the region, you should make room in your community for some of the poor from the city ghetto, so they can share its benefits. This will give your community, now segregated for a high-income group, a better balance of race and income, and will integrate your schools." Few will be so altruistic as to respond to that plea with enthusiasm.

It may make more sense to him to say, "Your community decided five years ago to do two things which are so inconsistent that they have not worked out. One was to maintain the 'character' of the community by two-acre residential zoning. The other was to zone the less desirable areas for commercial and industrial development, in the hope of increasing tax revenues without increasing school costs. One plant moved there, but its workers must commute long distances by car from the city. As soon as they can find other jobs near homes they can afford, they leave. This high labor turnover has made production so inefficient that the company is about to move away. Its experience has discouraged other firms from locating on your vacant land. If you will change part of your zoning to permit low income housing, the government will subsidize part of its cost, and will provide incentives for other industry to locate in your industrial area. If the new residents increase your school costs above the regional average, this will be equalized by the state." To the suburban taxpayer, the prospect of tax revenues from new business and industry may have a practical appeal which will overcome his aversion to some different neighbors, who will, after all, be workers with jobs.

These regional functions and the conditions caused by their failures have three characteristics which are relevant to the administrative mechanism we are seeking: First, the functions require joint action by several or all of the region's local governments. Second, a large part of their cost, and of the cost of relieving the conditions caused by their failure, must be provided by the Federal government, and to a lesser extent by the state governments. Third, both the functions and the conditions are so closely interrelated that they need to be administered as part of a plan for the region which takes them all into account.

These functions and conditions are not, of course, unique to the metropolitan regions. They constitute part of the fabric of life in each local community, in rural areas, and in the nation as a whole. The reason they command our present attention as regional questions is that the growth of the metropolitan region is a relatively new phenomenon, appearing in its present form in the last two decades, which has not been accompanied by the creation of administrative machinery able to cope with it. The absence of this machinery is causing much of the difficulty now observed in the administration of urban programs.

Let us now turn to the other side of this administrative question, the coordination of the Federal programs designed to support these functions and to treat these conditions.

There is no mystery surrounding the reasons why these Federal programs developed in a way which failed to bring the problems of the metropolitan region into focus. The Federal government first became involved in a major attack on poverty and unemployment in the Great Depression. The problem was then countrywide, not concentrated just in parts of the cities, or in isolated rural areas. Except in "The Regional Plan of New York and its Environs," published in 1929, the concept of the metropolitan region was not widely recognized. The Reconstruction Finance Corporation of the Hoover Administration, and the NRA, WPA, CCC, and housing and welfare programs of the New Deal, were necessarily designed to attack the problems on a national basis, with a series of separate new programs. This program approach has been encouraged since then by the nature of the legislative process, under which subjects are assigned to the various committees and subcommittees of the House and Senate. There are Senate Committees on Commerce, on Labor and Public Welfare, and on Public Works; House Committees on Inter-state and Foreign Commerce, Public Works, Banking and Currency, and on Education and Labor, with various subcommittees. There is as yet no Committee on Urban Affairs, though both Houses have Committees on Agriculture, which was a more pressing problem at a time when the cities seemed able to take care of themselves.

This legislative approach has continued up to the present time. It has resulted in a comparable separation of what we now recognize to be the interrelated parts of the total urban problem, as they were assigned to the major executive Departments: Housing and Urban Development; Health, Education and Welfare; Commerce; Labor; Justice; Transportation; and the Office of Economic Opportunity—and to the separate agencies within and outside these departments. Each of these agencies, in proposing new legislation and making budget requests to Congress, inevitably favors the partial solutions to the urban problem which are within its competence, and none is in a position to cope with the whole problem. The memorandum written by Douglas Costle in October, 1966, proposing a special Task Force to coordinate all Federal activities in Oakland, stated clearly what is needed:

The Federal government must face the total problem of the city and its residents and must administer its programs as if it were facing one problem with many aspects and many remedies, not many problems which happen to concern the same place and the same people.

Since, under the present system, each Federal agency is required to think of administration mainly in terms of the programs and problems assigned to it, there is as yet no place in the Federal government where one can "face the total problem of the city."

One other aspect of the Congressional attitude toward the cities should be noted here. The problems of housing, education, discrimination, employment, and poverty, now concentrated in the cities, exist also to a lesser degree in rural areas. The legislative solutions must be designed to reach them wherever they exist—in Appalachia as well as in Harlem, on an Indian reservation in Arizona as well as in the Flatlands of Oakland. It would seem evident that the complex interrelationships between these problems in a crowded urban ghetto require an administrative mechanism for coordinating Federal and local efforts more sophisticated than the mechanism needed in the Arizona desert or in the mined out hills of Appalachia. Yet here we find an interesting contrast in the actions taken.

227

A highly sophisticated planning and coordinating mechanism has been created by Congress for multistate rural areas in the form of the Appalachian Regional Commission, and the new Regional Action Planning Commissions being set up in the Ozarks, the Mesabi Range, New England, and the Four Corners area of the Southwest—and for a single state, sparsely settled, rural area in the Federal Field Committee for Alaska.

For the cities, however, Congress rejected even the limited mechanism for coordination proposed by the President in January, 1966, the Federal Coordinators provided in the original Demonstration Cities Bill. Instead, this was watered down to become the ineffective provision for Metropolitan Expediters which appears in the final Act. The reasons for this difference in approach are complex, and will be touched on later. Here, we need only to note that they do not include any widely held belief that urban areas have less need than rural areas of an effective coordinating mechanism to plan and administer large Federal programs.

This need is in fact recognized in most of the legislation dealing with the programs under review. The statutes establishing them are peppered with requirements for coordination and consultation between the various agencies responsible for: economic development; the anti-poverty program; training and education; housing and urban development; mass transportation; highway, airport, hospital, and library construction; air and water pollution control; conservation and parks; and probably other things. Many of these statutes recognize the existence of the metropolitan regions as essential planning units. They contain a variety of requirements that regional plans be adopted as a condition of Federal grants, or that Federal grants be consistent with such plans as exist.

None of these statutes, however, sets up any machinery for achieving Federal coordination, or for regional planning and action, in urban areas which is comparable to that provided for rural areas by the Appalachian Regional Commission and by the Regional Action Planning Commissions. The most recent statute, the "Model Cities and Metropolitan Development Act of 1966," contains a ringing declaration that "metropolitan areas are especially handicapped in this task by the complexity and scope of governmental services required in such rapidly growing areas, the multiplicity of political jurisdictions and agencies involved, and the inadequacy of the operational and administrative arrangements available for cooperation among them," and that "greater coordination of Federal programs and additional participation and cooperation are needed from the States and localities."

Disappointingly, the four operative sections which follow do little to achieve the declared purpose, though they do condition a variety of Federal grants on prior review by metropolitan regional planning agencies and provide for planning grants to such agencies. These are faltering steps in the right direction, but they fail to reach the goal.

The result of all this legislation is that, in each metropolitan region, the Federal government must now speak with many voices. Very often, these voices are ineffective and conflicting. In Oakland in 1966 there were one hundred and forty different programs and projects supported by Federal funding, administered by a dozen or more Federal, state, and city agencies. The local field representatives of the Federal agencies, or of the state agencies who spoke for them, were for the most part dedicated and experienced people, but each was low in his departmental hierarchy, many layers removed from those able to make policy.

As a result, with rare exceptions, they had no choice but to follow countrywide patterns set in Washington, with little opportunity to adapt these to local variations and needs. Few were able to rise above their departmental framework and see the whole picture in Oakland. If they did, there was little they could do about it.

The missing element in all this, obviously, is an official who can speak with authority for the entire Federal government in connection with all Federal programs in each city, as do the Federal Cochairmen in the Appalachian and Regional Action Planning Commissions. Since my experience in Oakland has a direct bearing on this question, it may be worthwhile to reexamine certain aspects of it.

I was retained simply as a consultant, with no other title or official position, and found that these were not needed. The announcement of Foley's backing, the urgency of Oakland's situation, and the statement that EDA would commit at least $15 million there, were enough to open all doors. In dealing with the Oakland community, with state officials in Sacramento, and with the local representatives of other Federal agencies, I was able to speak with the authority of the Assistant Secretary of Commerce in charge of the new program. I had ready access to him at all times, kept him fully informed, and was given a major voice in adapting EDA policies to meet local needs.

While I was responsible only for the EDA program, it was clear that the success of the EDA experiment would depend on close links with other Federal programs operating in Oakland.

To establish close relations with their local representatives, I met frequently and informally with almost all of them. We exchanged detailed information, and did all we could to reinforce each others' work. Throughout the year, I returned to Washington once or twice a month for consultation with EDA. While there, either through Foley, or on my own, acting as an independent consultant, I was able to see many of those at a policy-making level in the other agencies, in a way not usually possible for their local representatives in Oakland. To them, I explained the EDA experiment and urged that their agencies also move promptly in Oakland so the combination of all Federal programs would have maximum impact there.

The result of all this was that, with no job description or

official channels to hamper me, I found that I was in fact acting as a kind of overall Federal representative in Oakland. On the spot there, using the size and visibility of the EDA program as a magnet, there was much that I could do to draw together the efforts of all the Federal agencies. In Washington, where Oakland's problems had already attracted much attention, I could speak for Oakland on the basis of firsthand knowledge, and I could speak at the level where decisions were made.

The fact that this role of an overall Federal representative could be assumed so informally, almost accidentally, confirms the existence here of a real administrative vacuum. The favorable response to what I did, both in Oakland and in Washington, would indicate that this vacuum needs to be filled, and that, when this is done, it will be welcomed by all concerned.

Convinced by this experience, I began to urge, in Washington and elsewhere, that there was a need for a high-level Federal representative to speak for the entire government in its dealings with cities like Oakland or, preferably, with all the governments in each metropolitan region. In advancing this thought with others, both in and out of government, I have used the analogy of the way an ambassador represents our entire government in its dealings with a foregin government—or, more exactly, with a group of governments such as NATO or the Marshall Plan's OEEC, both of which I had observed closely as a member of the NATO international staff in 1951.

That analogy aroused, to my surprise, some opposition. This centered to a large extent on a feeling that we should not treat an area of this country as if it were a foreign nation, or set up a series of "Federal Mayors" who might diminish the authority of locally elected Mayors.

Obviously, the "foreign nation" argument is an emotional characterization which just serves to obscure the real issue. This is the fact that the financial interest of the Federal gov-

231

ernment in each large metropolitan region is far greater than it is in any foreign country. Further, if our urban programs are expanded to meet the actual needs, they will approach in most metropolitan regions the scale of the Marshall Plan and of NATO. The administrative problem is the same in each— how best to regulate the flow of large amounts of Federal funds, controlled by a variety of Federal agencies, to an area divided into separate governments whose close cooperation is needed to solve their common problems. In both the Marshall Plan and NATO, the solution adopted was to appoint a special ambassador to represent the United States Government in all its parts as a member of a council on which all the countries receiving United States aid for the solution of their common problems were represented. In practice, this worked out well.

In dealing with foreign countries, our government had long before learned that we could not afford to speak in them with many conflicting departmental voices. Instead, the ambassador, appointed by the President with the approval of Congress, must represent the whole government by presenting a coordinated policy, often hammered out with much difficulty first by the different departments in Washington. Representatives of those departments are attached to the staff of the ambassador, and their activities are coordinated by him. By the nature of his position, the ambassador has access to the highest officials and to private individuals in the country to which he is accredited, and one of his important duties is to make recommendations to Washington for adapting United States policy and actions to the needs and problems of that country.

This pattern was followed with the special ambassadors who served on the councils of the governments who were members of the Marshall Plan and of NATO. In those complex situations, the United States was also represented by a separate ambassador to each member government. Nothing of that sort is suggested here for the metropolitan regions within the country, where a single representative to the group of governments constituting the region is all that is needed.

Since the use of an ambassador as a high-level representative has been found so necessary in coordinating departmental activities in other countries and groups of countries, is there any reason to suppose that a similar device is not needed and would not work in handling the massive urban programs now in prospect here? Certainly no one who has observed an effective embassy in operation would seriously propose that the country would be better served if the ambassador were limited to representing the State Department, and the representatives of Defense, AID, Labor, Commerce, Treasury, and the CIA were all turned loose to operate on their own—though each of those departments may occasionally long for this, and the last named seems sometimes to do more of this than is wise.

The Mayors of several large cities objected to the limited form of high-level representation, the Federal Coordinator, proposed in the Demonstration Cities Bill by the President in January, 1966. Apparently they felt that it would diminish either their prestige or their effectiveness not to continue to deal with the Federal government through a multiplicity of lower-level representatives, using political channels when available for direct appeals to the White House or to powerful members of Congress. This is not a persuasive attitude, when the stakes involved are the effective handling of billions of dollars of Federal funds to resolve a major national crisis.

The Mayor of Oakland, John Reading, who perhaps could be more objective because these political channels were not open to him, and whose experience in dealing with major Federal programs was more extensive than that of most Mayors, appealed urgently in Washington for a "Federal czar in Oakland, who can direct all of these programs, and with whom we can deal directly, on a clear line of authority."

The availability of a high-level Federal official to deal directly with local Mayors on behalf of the entire Federal gov-

233

ernment would not, as some critics have suggested, be substituting a "Federal Mayor" for the local ones. On the contrary, the authority of the local Mayors, and their ability to solve the problems of their communities, would be greatly enhanced by dealing with such an official on all Federal and regional questions.

We are now ready to return to our initial question: What administrative mechanism can best coordinate the action of Federal, state, and local agencies by controlling the flow of Federal funds to support urban programs?

With respect to the local governments in each region, it is evident that their role in the performance of regional functions is now inhibited by the lack of a central administrative mechanism, a forum where they, together with the state and Federal governments, can meet to plan and direct the flow of funds required for these regional functions. The need of such a forum for programs treating the conditions in each locality is less pressing, but the close relation between all these programs indicates an advantage in handling them together.

For the Federal programs, we have suggested that the multiplicity of channels be brought together in each region by a single high-level official representing the whole government.

With these points in mind, we can now state the question in more detail. It is:

Can we combine, in one administrative mechanism, adequate representation for the Federal, state, and local governments to plan and direct the flow of all their funds to support these regional functions, and at the same time to provide remedies for the conditions created by past failures?

This question has already been answered by Congress for rural regions, each made up of several states, by setting up the Appalachian Regional Commission, under the Appalachian Regional Development Act of 1965, and the Regional Action Planning Commissions, under Title V of the Public Works and Economic Development Act of 1965. Congress also stated the need for a comparable mechanism in metropolitan regions, with clarity and urgency, in Section 201 of the Model Cities and Metropolitan Development Act of 1966, quoted above on page 229, but then failed to provide it.

Following this lead, the answer to our question seems clear: Appropriate legislation should be passed to provide similar Action Planning Commissions in the metropolitan regions, adapted to the more complex and varied government patterns which they contain.

Our examination of these questions indicates that the salient features of such legislation, following the basic pattern of Title V of the Public Works and Economic Development Act of 1965, should be:

1) Responsibility for setting up and supporting the Metropolitan Action Planning Commissions should be centered at a high level in Washington. Some feel that the logical place for this would be in the Bureau of the Budget, since the main work of the Federal Cochairman of each Commission would be in the fields of planning, budgeting, and administration. Foley, in his recent book, *The Achieving Ghetto,* argues that the viewpoint of the Budget Bureau is too narrow, and that a new Presidential Policy Group should be set up to provide a more widely representative national planning agency. Either seems preferable to placing them in the Department of Housing and Urban Development, whose responsibility for operating part of the Federal urban programs would bring it into conflict with the Federal agencies responsible for the other parts. There is much to be said on both sides. Any solution should work out well enough in practice. Wherever they are located, the planning support for metropolitan regions provided by Title II of the Model Cities and Metropolitan Development Act of 1966 should be placed in the same agency.

2) The definition of a Metropolitan Region should be the "standard metropolitan statistical area" established by the

Bureau of the Budget, which is used in the Model Cities Act, with modifications where justified by local situations.

3) The state or states in which each region lies should designate the way the local governments are to be represented on the Commission, following guidelines established in the statute. To hold the Commissions to manageable size, these guidelines would have to limit membership to the larger cities and counties of the region, with counties representing the smaller towns. Precedents for this already exist in various councils of local governments such as the Association of Bay Area Governments for the San Francisco area. These bodies, formed to bring local governments together to discuss common problems, could become the foundation for the new Commissions in those regions. The New York City metropolitan region presents a special problem, because of its tremendous size and the fact that it lies in three states. There, the best vehicle would appear to be the Executive Committee of the Tristate Transportation Commission, which includes representatives of the three states, New York, New Jersey, and Connecticut, and of New York City. The provision for local membership on each Commission should be flexible enough to adapt to the special circumstances of each region, but enable the Federal government to make a firm decision if the state and local governments could not agree.

4) The Federal member of each Commission should be a Federal Cochairman, appointed by the President with the advice and consent of the Senate, with the rank of an Assistant Secretary of a cabinet department. His affirmative vote would be required for any decision of the Commission relating to a Federal program.

5) Similarly, each State in which the region is located should have a Cochairman as a member, whose affirmative vote would be required for any decision of the Commission which affected programs of his state.

6) With the required concurring votes of the Federal and

state Cochairmen, decisions would be taken by majority vote of the local governments represented on the Commission, with their votes weighted according to their population. In metropolitan regions, a weighted vote would be more fair than the single vote given to each state on the rural Regional Commissions. Where the weighted vote would give one city a dominant position, provision could be made for a higher percentage vote or a veto on some questions to protect the smaller members. Here again, a special provision would be needed for the Commission in the New York City metropolitan region, to accommodate the three States involved and to give adequate representation to the smaller municipalities. The same would be needed in other multi-state regions, and possibly in others dominated by a single large city.

7) A mechanism should be set up for coordinating all Federal programs and agencies through the Federal Cochairmen which is more specific than the provision in Title V, which simply says, "In matters coming before a regional commission, the Federal Cochairman shall, to the extent practicable, consult with the Federal departments and agencies having an interest in the subject matter." At the local level, a good model for this is provided in the Critical Urban Problems Steering Committee of the Federal Executive Board in the San Francisco area, used as part of the Oakland experiment. In Washington, the procedures which have been developed by the existing Cochairmen should be helpful.

8) The functions of the Commissions could to a large extent duplicate those provided in Title V for the Regional Action Planning Commissions. These include (Section 503): the preparation of long-range development programs; promoting increased private investment; preparing legislative and other recommendations for Federal, state, and local agencies; and providing a forum for consideration of regional problems.

9) In the urban regions, advantage could be taken of the existence of stronger local governments and the wide variety

237

of local leadership to eliminate what is now the most cumbersome and annoying element in the relation between the local and Federal governments, the administration of each program by the approval of projects in Washington. Decentralization of project approval by delegation of authority to local agencies has been accomplished to a considerable extent by the Poverty Program and by some other agencies. When the size of the urban programs increases, the need for decentralization will be much greater. The machinery of the new Commissions could be used to provide this in a consistent and coordinated manner for all agencies by taking three simple steps:

First, each Federal department and agency could be required to allocate to the Commission for each metropolitan region a proportionate share of its appropriation for urban programs, on a basis reflecting the proportion of the need for that program in each region. This would work best if the allocation were made as part of a national plan for the most effective utilization of all resources.

Second, the Commission could then allocate appropriations to the cities and counties of the region on a basis consistent with need, but with appropriate modifications to reflect decisions reached in its regional planning.

Third, a local Project Board could be set up in each city and county of the region, made up of local officials and Federal and state representatives, to approve all individual projects within the established limits of budget and plan.

This procedure would enable the local communities to select the projects best suited to local needs, without encountering the delays and difficulties now experienced in sending them on to Washington for approval. In doing so, they could make full use of the local knowledge and ideas available in business organizations, in labor unions, and in the Poverty Program community action committees. The same procedure might be followed for state programs.

The creation of Regional Commissions along these lines

238

would provide a much needed forum for dealing with the urgent urban questions outlined in this and the preceding chapter. They would provide a Federal focus on the total urban problem that is now lacking, together with a similar focus for each state involved. The local governments would become part of the regional planning and action process in a way not now possible, and would be given a much more meaningful role in adapting Federal and state programs to local needs.

In this connection, it should be noted that for forty years the lead in planning for metropolitan regions has been taken by a private organization, the Regional Plan Association of New York, with foundation and business support. Similar independent, citizen-led, professional planning agencies, modeled on Regional Plan, could, with government financial support, become the principal planning arms of the Regional Action Planning Commissions.

Before ending this discussion of administrative questions, another point should be made. This is, that the emphasis here on the role of government should not be taken to indicate that these regional functions are solely the responsibility of government, or even that the role of government in them is the dominant one. Neither is the case.

The major part of the cost of these functions, and of the action taken to perform them, is provided by the private sector. In economic development, for example, the $65 billion spent annually by business and industry for new plant and equipment far exceeds, in its effect on employment, anything that government can do. The same is true of housing, of transportation, of the disposal of industrial waste. Even in planning, business and industry devote more time, money, and effort to planning which affects the development of metropolitan regions than is needed by all the governments involved.

The role of government in this field is a limited, but extremely important, one. It is to influence the multitude of decisions of the private sector through comprehensive planning, incentives, regulation, zoning, and public investment.

Since our subject is the administrative mechanism needed by government for that purpose, it has received our attention rather than the role of the private sector. It is important to remember, however, that the principal measure of the success of the government mechanism we are seeking will be its ability to mobilize private resources and action in the performance of their larger share in all these funtcions. This is a formidable task. By comparison to those of government, the administrative mechanisms of the private sector are vast, numerous, and effective. They operate internally in the giant corporations: General Motors, Standard Oil, A. T. & T., IBM, Federated Department Stores, Sears, Safeway—to name but a few out of many—and in the banks, insurance companies, and utilities. They include trade associations, many with a strong regional orientation, in almost every field of business and industry, chambers of commerce, labor unions, universities, religious organizations, conservation groups, and others. There are many directed specifically at urban problems: settlement houses, legal aid societies, the Urban League, Urban America, the Urban Coalition, and the Regional Plan Association.

In numbers of people involved, in dollars spent, in the variety of their activities, the impact of all these private mechanisms on the decisions which shape each metropolitan region will always far exceed the impact of the Federal, state, and local governments combined.

The importance of the government role is that it can, one may hope, guide and influence these decisions of the private sector in a way that will enable our great metropolitan regions to function so effectively that their present urgent problems will be solved.

To accomplish this, the need for improvement of the administration of our Federal urban programs is immediate and pressing. Prompt Congressional action to establish Metropolitan Region Action Planning Commissions along the lines suggested would require only modest administrative budgets, compared to the cost of the urban programs now in force. Once established, with authority to channel the flow of Federal funds into their regions, they could immediately begin to improve the handling of existing programs. As they gained experience in this, they could rapidly become the most useful source of information and advice to the administration and to Congress on what is needed in the way of new and larger programs.

Two years have passed since the events described in this book—years in which the urban ghettos of America have continued to decay and burn. Therefore this book must end with no conclusion, for none is now available. It must end with a question: Can this nation now, at the peak of its power and success, fail to muster the massive resources, and to create the fresh ideas, needed to respond to the cry of its cities?

Index

245

246

247